Storyteller

GENESIS

THE BEGINNING

Storyteller

GENESIS

THE BEGINNING

Lifeway Press®
Brentwood, Tennessee

Editorial Team

Rob Tims
Devotional Writer

Tyler Quillet
Managing Editor

Stephanie Cross
Associate Editor

Joel Polk
Publisher, Small Group Publishing

Reid Patton
Senior Editor

John Paul Basham
Director, Adult Ministry Publishing

Jon Rodda
Art Director

CONTENTS

THE STORYTELLER SERIES

God could've chosen to reveal Himself in any way He desired, yet in His wisdom, He chose to reveal Himself in the context of a story. We come to know and understand this reality as we immerse ourselves in the Scriptures and begin to see the entirety of Scripture as one interconnected story. By becoming familiar with the individual stories of Scripture, we train ourselves to see each as one part of God's big story.

Storyteller is a series of devotional and group Bible study experiences designed to take people through Scripture in a way that is beautiful, intuitive, and interactive. Each volume uses a book of the Bible or a portion of Scripture from within a book to examine a key theme. This theme guides the Bible study experience and gives readers handles to help understand and digest what they're reading.

At the end of each study, your should have a deeper understanding of God, His Word, the big themes of Scripture, the connectedness of God's story, and His work in your life.

Let's enter the story together.

ABOUT GENESIS

The book of Genesis takes its name from the Greek version of the Old Testament (the Septuagint), which called it Genesis (Greek Gk *Geneseos*), meaning "of birth"—a reference to Genesis 2:4.

AUTHOR

Since pre-Christian times authorship of the Torah, the five books that include the book of Genesis, has been attributed to Moses. Even though Genesis is technically anonymous, both the Old and New Testaments unanimously recognize Moses as the Torah's author.

BACKGROUND

The first five books of the Bible are known as the Torah (a Hebrew term for "law" or "instruction") or the Pentateuch (literally, five vessels). Genesis, the first book of the Torah, provides both the universal history of humankind and the patriarchal history of the nation of Israel. The first section (chaps. 1–11) is a general history commonly called the "primeval history," showing how all humanity descended from one couple and became sinners. The second section (chaps. 12–50) is a more specific history commonly referred to as the "patriarchal history," focusing on the covenant God made with Abraham and his descendants: Isaac, Jacob, and Jacob's twelve sons. Genesis unfolds God's plan to bless and redeem humanity through Abraham's descendants. The book concludes with the events that led to the Israelites being in the land of Egypt.

DATE

Moses is the central figure of the next four books of the Pentateuch (Exodus, Leviticus, Numbers, and Deuteronomy). He is not featured in Genesis and lived many years after the events described. Moses likely wrote these down sometime between 1500 BC and 1300 BC. Prior to Moses writing it down, the history and story.

KEY THEMES

Genesis has several key themes that are important throughout the rest of the Bible.

CREATION: Genesis introduces God as the sovereign Lord and Creator of all things. God created everything out of nothing. He is separate from the created order, and no part of creation is to be considered an extension of God.

HUMAN LIFE: Adam and Eve were created in the image of God, unique from the rest of creation, to have fellowship with God. All human beings at every age and every state bear the image of God and are also born with a sinful nature inherited from Adam and Eve.

SIN: Adam and Eve chose freely to disobey God, fell from innocence, and lost their freedom. Their sinful nature has passed to every other human being. Sin resulted in death, both physical and spiritual. Sin has led to a world of pain and struggle.

COVENANT: Genesis first introduces the idea of covenants. Genesis is a narrative of relationships, and certainly relationships grounded in covenants with God. These covenants provide a unifying principle for understanding the whole of Scripture and define the relationship between God and man.[1] For more see page 148.

WHY STUDY GENESIS?

The book of Genesis is the great book of beginnings. Genesis permits us to view the beginning of a multitude of realities that shape our daily existence: the creation of the universe and the planet earth; the origins of plant and animal life; and the origins of human beings, marriage, families, nations, industry, artistic expression, religious ritual, prophecy, sin, law, crime, conflict, punishment, and death.

Genesis lays the groundwork for everything else we read and experience in Scripture. Through Genesis we understand where we came from, how we got in the fallen state we are in, and the beginnings of God's gracious work on our behalf. Genesis unfolds God's original purpose for humanity.

Genesis provides the foundation from which we understand God's covenant with Israel that was established with the giving of the law. For the Israelite community, the stories of the origins of humanity, sin, and the covenant relationship with God helped them understand why God gave them the law.

It helps us understand where we came from, what went wrong, and how God has a plan to redeem the world through Jesus Christ, who is the Son of Abraham.

OUTLINE OF GENESIS 1-11

I. Creation of Heaven and Earth (1:1–2:3)

    A. Creator and creation (1:1–2)

    B. Six days of creation (1:3–31)

    C. Seventh day—day of consecration (2:1–3)

II. The Human Family in and outside the Garden (2:4–4:26)

    A. The man and woman in the garden (2:4–25)

    B. The man and woman expelled from the garden (3:1–24)

    C. Adam and Eve's family outside the garden (4:1–26)

III. Adam's Family Line (5:1–6:8)

    A. Introduction: Creation and blessing (5:1–2)

    B. "Image of God" from Adam to Noah (5:3–32)

    C. Conclusion: Procreation and perversion (6:1–8)

IV. Noah and His Family (6:9–9:29)

    A. Righteous Noah and the corrupt world (6:9–12)

    B. Coming judgment but the ark of promise (6:13–7:10)

    C. Worldwide flood of judgment (7:11–24)

    D. God's remembrance and rescue of Noah (8:1–14)

    E. Exiting the ark (8:15–19)

    F. Worship and the word of promise (8:20–22)

    G. God's covenant with the new world (9:1–17)

    H. Noah's sons and future blessing (9:18–29)

V. The Nations and the Tower of Babylon (10:1–11:26)

    A. Table of Nations (10:1–32)

    B. Tower of Babylon (11:1–9)

    C. Family line of Abram (11:10–26)[2]

HOW TO USE THIS STUDY

Each week follows a repeated rhythm to guide you in your study of Genesis
and was crafted with lots of white space and photographic imagery to facilitate
a time of reflection on Scripture.

The week begins with an
introduction to the themes
of the week. Throughout
each week you'll find
Scripture readings, devotions,
and beautiful imagery
to guide your time.

WEEK 1

CREATION

Each week includes five days
of Scripture reading along with
a short devotional thought
and three questions to process
what you've read.

The Scripture reading is printed
out for you with plenty of
space for you to take notes,
circle, underline, and interact
with the passage.

The sixth day contains no reading beyond a couple of verses to give you time to pause and listen to what God has said through the Scriptures this week. You may be tempted to skip this day all together, but resist this temptation. Sit and be quiet with God—even if it's only for a few minutes.

The seventh day each week offers a list of open-ended questions that apply to any passage of Scripture. Use this day to reflect on your own or meet with a group to discuss what you've learned. Take intentional time to remember and reflect on what the story of Genesis is teaching you.

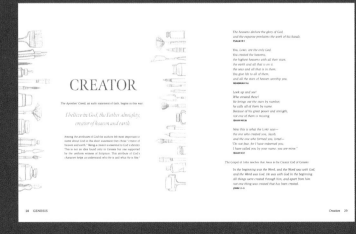

Throughout each week of study, you will notice callout boxes or supplemental pages provided to give greater context and clarity to the Scripture you're reading. These features will help you connect the story of Genesis to the bigger story of Scripture.

LEADING A GROUP

Each week of study contains a set of questions that can be used for small group meetings. These open-ended questions are meant to guide discussion of the week's Scripture passage. No matter the size of your group, here are some helpful tips for guiding discussion.

PREPARE

REVIEW the Scripture and your answers to the week's questions ahead of time.

PRAY over your group as well as the Scriptures you've been studying. Ask God's Spirit for help to lead the group deeper into God's truth and deeper in relationship with one another.

MINIMIZE DISTRACTIONS

We live in a time when our attention is increasingly divided. Try to see your group time as a space and respite from the digital clutter—from scrolling, notifications, likes, and newsfeeds. Commit to one another to give focused time and attention to the discussion at hand and minimize outside distractions. Help people focus on what's most important: connecting with God, with the Bible, and with one another.

ENCOURAGE DISCUSSION

A good small group experience has the following characteristics.

EVERYONE IS INCLUDED. Your goal is to foster a community where people are welcome just as they are but encouraged to grow spiritually.

EVERYONE PARTICIPATES. Encourage everyone to ask questions, share, or read aloud.

NO ONE DOMINATES. Even though you may be "leading" the group, try to see yourself as a participant steering the conversation rather than a teacher imparting information.

DON'T RUSH. Don't feel that a moment of silence is a bad thing. People may need time, and we should be glad to give it to them. Don't feel like you have to ask all the questions or stay away from questions that aren't included. Be sensitive to the Holy Spirit and to one another. Take your time.

INPUT IS AFFIRMED AND FOLLOWED UP. Make sure you point out something true or helpful in a response. Don't just move on. Build community with follow-up questions, asking other people to share when they have experienced similar things or how a truth has shaped their understanding of God and the Scripture you're studying. Conversation stalls when people feel that you don't want to hear their answers or that you're looking for only a certain answer. Engagement and affirmation keeps the conversation going.

GOD AND HIS WORD ARE CENTRAL. The questions in this study are meant to steer the conversation back to God, His Word, and the work of the gospel in our lives. Opinions and experiences are valuable and can be helpful, but God is the center of the Bible, the center of our story, and should be the center of our discussion. Trust Him to lead the discussion. Continually point people to the Word and to active steps of faith.

KEEP CONNECTING

Spiritual growth occurs in the context of community. Think of ways to connect with group members during the week. Your group will be more enjoyable the more you get to know one another through time spent outside of an official group meeting. The more people are comfortable with and involved in one another's lives, the more they'll look forward to being together. When people move beyond being friendly to truly being friends who form a community, they come to each session eager to engage instead of merely attending. Reserve time each week to touch base with individual group members.

WEEK 1

CREATION

Every story has a beginning.

Human beings have long sought to understand how the universe came to be. Many people groups from ancient times recorded their ideas and stories about the origins of the world. These varied accounts share many similarities, yet none truly compare to the creation account of Genesis.

Only Genesis claims that all the world exists due to the work of a single God and that God continues to maintain its existence. Only Genesis instructs readers to glory in the God who made the marvelous things we see, not deify and worship those things. Only Genesis puts an enormously high value on human beings, stating that men and women are made in God's very image.

What separated Genesis from other creation accounts millennia ago separates it from atheistic and scientific theories in our day. These hypotheses presume that all life and matter originated from the primordial conditions of the early universe and the processes that unfolded over time. In contrast, Genesis gives credit to the will and word of God for the world's existence and shows that God created the world with purpose and intent.

We should not expect the opening verses of Genesis to answer specific scientific questions we might have about the earth's origins. The book of Genesis is more like a hymn, poem, or song—it is not at all like a scientific textbook or philosophical muse. Instead, we should read it and marvel at the transcendent mystery of God as Creator and consider the worldview implications as we do. We will learn something about how creation came to be, but more importantly, why it came to be.

Let's begin at the beginning.

GENESIS 1:1-5

THE CREATION

1 In the beginning God created the heavens and the earth.
² Now the earth was formless and empty, darkness covered the surface of the watery depths, and the Spirit of God was hovering over the surface of the waters. ³ Then God said, "Let there be light," and there was light. ⁴ God saw that the light was good, and God separated the light from the darkness. ⁵ God called the light "day," and the darkness he called "night." There was an evening, and there was a morning: one day.

<table>
<tr><td>DAY
1</td></tr>
</table>

THE FIRST DAY

While the creation account of Genesis 1 may not be scientific, it is direct and clear. Straight away, we are forced to reckon with divine truths that shape our view of the world. Namely, the whole world was created by the will and word of the God of the Bible. To do this, He purposefully turned chaos into order.

He alone is the Creator who has great freedom and power to speak matter into existence out of nothing. Prior to this, He alone existed. He co-exists with this world only because He chose to create it. This is not a deity who goes to battle with other so-called gods or with any aspects of His creation like we might find in other ancient origin stories. As the apostle Paul told those gathered in Areopagus centuries later, "The God who made the world and everything in it—he is Lord of heaven and earth—does not live in shrines made by hands. Neither is he served by human hands, as though he needed anything, since he himself gives everyone life and breath and all things" (Acts 17:24-25).

This God made the heavens and the earth. To believe the earth exists due to God's speech is one thing, but to believe that the heavens are His creative handiwork as well is quite another. This is not merely a reference to what we might call our atmosphere and the universe's many wonders—this also includes the unseen spiritual realm where God and the angels dwell. God spoke His own realm into reality.

God created time itself. This alone should lead us to wonder. Though God has no beginning, His creation does. Time is the first of God's chosen tools for bringing order out of chaos. With the creation of periods of light and darkness, chaos is given its first boundaries, and we are given yet another reason to marvel.

The world only exists because
God chose to create it.

REFLECTIONS

God is eternal and stands outside of time and creation. How does reflecting on God's "otherness" affect your view of Him?

Why would God, who does not need anything, make the world to begin with?

How does what we believe about the way the world came to exist affect the way we view the world?

INSIGHT

God created the world out of nothing. Theologians called this *ex-nihilo,* which comes from the Latin meaning "out of nothing." Prior to creation, God was all that existed. He is eternal and, therefore, timeless. While this might be a lot to wrap our minds around, it's meant to feel that way. Though God is infinite and beyond what we can fully comprehend, God is knowable because He has chosen to make Himself known.

GENESIS 1:6-13

[6] Then God said, "Let there be an expanse between the waters, separating water from water." [7] So God made the expanse and separated the water under the expanse from the water above the expanse. And it was so. [8] God called the expanse "sky." Evening came and then morning: the second day.

[9] Then God said, "Let the water under the sky be gathered into one place, and let the dry land appear." And it was so. [10] God called the dry land "earth," and the gathering of the water he called "seas." And God saw that it was good. [11] Then God said, "Let the earth produce vegetation: seed-bearing plants and fruit trees on the earth bearing fruit with seed in it according to their kinds." And it was so. [12] The earth produced vegetation: seed-bearing plants according to their kinds and trees bearing fruit with seed in it according to their kinds. And God saw that it was good. [13] Evening came and then morning: the third day.

<table>
<tr><td>DAY
2</td><td></td></tr>
</table>

THE SECOND
AND THIRD DAY

Whereas Genesis 1:1-5 establishes God as the Creator and His creation of time as the first function of bringing order to chaos, verses 6-13 introduce two other major functions of creation that further His ordering work: weather and agriculture. God intentionally designed the world so that plants bear seeds and seeds grow into new plants, and the waters are the precipitation that plays such a crucial role in sustaining and promoting life. He is not only the Creator of life—He is also the Sustainer of life.

Individuals who have spent a significant amount of time living in more rural environments likely have a better understanding of what it is like to "live with the land." To wake with the sunrise and rest with the sunset in every season, to plant and harvest crops and eat what is available in those seasons, to pray for rain and against famine—such is life for those who farm and provide food for the world.

God saw what He had made and called it "good." The shifting of seasons and of time and the rhythms of life inherent to the natural world are irrefutably good. That God saw that all of this was good means it all operates according to the purpose of His design.

Everything God does and everything God makes is good because He good. And we can see that in the very first days of the world. The cycle of life and growth are already identifiable and traceable here at the beginning. These verses compel us to reflect on the pace and rhythms of our life as well as the One who gave us life.

Everything God makes is good
because He is good.

REFLECTIONS

What ways do we see God's order and purpose on display in His world other than nature?

How are you embracing living within the rhythms of God's good creation?

How does trying to live apart from the cycles and functions God gave creation create stress and chaos in our lives?

CREATOR

The Apostles' Creed, an early statement of faith, begins in this way:

*I believe in God, the Father almighty,
creator of heaven and earth.*

Among the attributes of God the authors felt most important to name about God in this short statement they chose "creator of heaven and earth." Being a creator is essential to God's identity. This is not an idea found only in Genesis but one supported by the uniform witness of Scripture. This attribute of God's character helps us understand who He is and what He is like.[3]

The heavens declare the glory of God,
and the expanse proclaims the work of his hands.
PSALM 19:1

You, LORD, are the only God.
You created the heavens,
the highest heavens with all their stars,
the earth and all that is on it,
the seas and all that is in them.
You give life to all of them,
and all the stars of heaven worship you.
NEHEMIAH 9:6

Look up and see!
Who created these?
He brings out the stars by number;
he calls all of them by name.
Because of his great power and strength,
not one of them is missing.
ISAIAH 40:26

Now this is what the LORD says—
the one who created you, Jacob,
and the one who formed you, Israel—
"Do not fear, for I have redeemed you;
I have called you by your name; you are mine."
ISAIAH 43:1

The Gospel of John teaches that Jesus is the Creator God of Genesis:

In the beginning was the Word, and the Word was with God,
and the Word was God. He was with God in the beginning.
All things were created through him, and apart from him
not one thing was created that has been created.
JOHN 1:1–3

GENESIS 1:14-15

[14] Then God said, "Let there be lights in the expanse of the sky to separate the day from the night. They will serve as signs for seasons and for days and years. [15] They will be lights in the expanse of the sky to provide light on the earth." And it was so.

<table>
<tr><td>DAY
3</td><td># THE FOURTH
AND FIFTH DAY</td></tr>
</table>

The journey through the story of creation swings wildly from the vastness of space to the depths of the oceans in days four and five.

On day four, we realize God was not necessarily making something every day but was speaking every day. God created by speaking, but in speaking, He was not always creating matter. In verses 14-19, He was creating function. These luminaries (the sun, moon, and stars) already existed with the creation of the heavens and the earth and time in verses 1-3. But in this passage, God gave them the functions of marking time: day, night, seasons, and years.

While the celestial bodies receive special attention in the creation story because they serve the purpose of marking time, the waters of the earth receive special attention because the creatures in them get singled out in this narrative in a way that others forms of animate life do not—except human beings, of course. The oceans remain a marvelous mystery to the most dedicated and well-equipped scientists even to this day. Yet the clear intent of the writer is to communicate that even the mysteries of the deep owe their existence to this sovereign Creator and are not to be worshiped as idols or feared as something beyond His control. Rather God's total governance of the world should lead us into awe and wonder.

Interestingly, the first recorded blessing in the Bible was issued to the first living being created (v. 22). It is their great privilege to fill the waters and the sky. They need God's blessing to make life because only God's word brings life. With a word, God brought these creatures into existence, and with the additional word of a blessing, God gave them assurance of continued existence.

God's total governance of the world should
lead us into awe and wonder.

REFLECTIONS

Which is the more compelling area of interest to you: space or the ocean? Why? How might learning more about these areas lead you to worship God?

What parts of nature do you sometimes fail to appreciate as part of God's good work? Why?

Recognizing that God has blessed the animal kingdom, how should humans relate to these creatures?

INSIGHT

Days one, two, and three of creation involve God forming the earth and causing the unproductive to become productive. Days four, five, and six involve filling the earth He formed. What was uninhabited became inhabited with life.

GENESIS 1:24–31

[24] Then God said, "Let the earth produce living creatures according to their kinds: livestock, creatures that crawl, and the wildlife of the earth according to their kinds." And it was so. [25] So God made the wildlife of the earth according to their kinds, the livestock according to their kinds, and all the creatures that crawl on the ground according to their kinds. And God saw that it was good.

[26] Then God said, "Let us make man in our image, according to our likeness. They will rule the fish of the sea, the birds of the sky, the livestock, the whole earth, and the creatures that crawl on the earth."

[27]   So God created man in his own image;

he created him in the image of God;

he created them male and female.

[28] God blessed them, and God said to them, "Be fruitful, multiply, fill the earth, and subdue it. Rule the fish of the sea, the birds of the sky, and every creature that crawls on the earth." [29] God also said, "Look, I have given you every seed-bearing plant on the surface of the entire earth and everay tree whose fruit contains seed. This will be food for you, [30] for all the wildlife of the earth, for every bird of the sky, and for every creature that crawls on the earth — everything having the breath of life in it — I have given every green plant for food." And it was so. [31] God saw all that he had made, and it was very good indeed. Evening came and then morning: the sixth day.

<table>
<tr><td>DAY
4</td><td></td></tr>
</table>

THE SIXTH DAY

We can't read Genesis 1:24-31 without wondering at its implications for human beings. This passage is one of the most insightful texts in all of Scripture and serves as a foundational building block for understanding the God who created us and what it means to be a human being.

First we learn that human beings are made in the image of God, which tells us something about ourselves and something about God. Notice the use of the plural in verse 26: "Let *us* make man in *our* image, after *our* likeness." Understanding what it means to be made in God's image in some ways hinges on whether the writer of Genesis and his audience were already aware of some type of plurality in the person of God—what we now know as the Trinity.

A closer reading of verse 27 seems to support the idea that the writer did have such a belief. Twice he tells us that human beings were created in God's image, and at the third mention, he highlighted their being created "male and female." The single human being (for we are all human) is created as a plurality that reflects God's own singularity and plurality. Gender is more than biology; it reflects the very nature of God.

Second, God gave human beings a task. Like the creatures made before us, we are also blessed to reproduce but also to serve as caretakers over the other living creatures blessed to grow in number. Human beings are to possess a love for all forms of life and treasure the whole earth. Through their care, God provides the food needed for human beings to thrive.

Human beings subdue and rule the earth but not in a domineering or flippant way. We are to image God by bringing order and functioning as sub-creators. We are to loving tend the world God made as His representatives.

This, God says, is "very good indeed" (v. 31).

God created us and defines what it
means to be a human being.

REFLECTIONS

What does it teach us about ourselves to know every human being is made in the image of God?

What are some ways the idea of being made in God's image is distorted today?

What are the implications for human identity, particularly as it relates to gender, given this text?

GENESIS 2:1-3

2 So the heavens and the earth and everything in them were completed. [2] On the seventh day God had completed his work that he had done, and he rested on the seventh day from all his work that he had done. [3] God blessed the seventh day and declared it holy, for on it he rested from all his work of creation.

THE SEVENTH DAY

Perhaps you can relate to the sense of satisfaction and closure that comes when you've completed a major project, be it one that took several years (such as a degree) or several hours (such as gardening). With the work done, you can cease your effort and enjoy all the good that comes with its completion. This is the glimpse of God in Genesis 2:1-3. God's very good work was finished, so He stopped creating.

Three times in three verses the writer says some version of, "God did not work." After all of His creation work, God rested. God is pictured as creating to achieve the rest. Day seven of creation is not the appendix but the resolution to the creation story. That God blessed the day in the same way He blessed animals and humans tells us everything we need to know about the significance of this day and the importance of rest.

But how are we to rest? Even the theologically and biblically informed opinions vary, and each of those has many shades. The biblical practice of observing rest is called Sabbath. All forms of practicing Sabbath give us time and space to acknowledge the supremacy of God. To ignore Sabbath rest is to miss out on knowing and worshiping God.

Taking a Sabbath rest allows our bodies and minds to refresh, but our very need to rest also makes us keenly aware of the distinction between us and God. Rest is an opportunity for us to trust God to keep and sustain us as we cease from our labors.

When God's work was complete,
He ceased creating and rested.

REFLECTIONS

How are you currently practicing the blessing of Sabbath?

What aspects of life most frequently or most powerfully tempt you to neglect practicing the Sabbath in some way?

Do you view rest as something to look forward to or something you have to do? How does this passage inform the way you should view rest?

PAUSE & LISTEN

Spend some time reflecting over the week's reading.

In the beginning God created
the heavens and the earth.

GENESIS 1:1

REFLECTION

Use these questions for personal reflection or group discussion on Genesis 1.

What stuck out to you most in this week's reading? What surprised you? Confused you?

What does this week's Scripture teach you about God and His character?

What does this week's Scripture teach you about humanity and our need for grace?

What do the origins of life, as described by the Bible, teach us about the meaning of life?

What steps of faith and obedience is God asking you to take through these Scriptures?

PRAY

God thank You for being the Creator of all that exists. We praise You for filling and sustaining us, even now.

WEEK 2

CREATURES

We bear God's image.

Cruising at a high altitude in a commercial airplane over the eastern United States on a sunny, cloudless day, you can look down and easily identify a number of forests. Some of them are small and some of them are quite large, but their groupings are indistinguishable from your vantage point. It is simply impossible to "miss the forest for the trees," and you know individual trees make up the forests you admire.

Such is the literary vantage point that Genesis 1 provides regarding the creation of the universe. You are given a view of God's work on a grand scale, and you know that if you could get closer to it, you could see more of the details.

Genesis 2 gives you a closer look. The narrative of Genesis 2:4-25 emerges as a more detailed view of how life came to be on the earth. More specifically, we learn about human beings and their place in God's creation. It's as if the writer understood that we would want to know more about ourselves, so he zoomed in on the grand narrative to show us our origin story.

We desperately need a deeper understanding of what it means to be human beings. Postmodern philosophies teach us to create our own meaning and purpose and that anything we find worthwhile is more than adequate to legitimize our existence. When we allow people to determine their own meaning, it shatters a meaningful community that the common grace of being made in the image of God gives all of human life. Read Genesis 2 prayerfully and with great care, considering the ways it can speak to the brokenness we experience in our world today, individually and in community.

GENESIS 2:4-7

MAN AND WOMAN IN THE GARDEN

[4] These are the records of the heavens and the earth, concerning their creation. At the time that the LORD God made the earth and the heavens, [5] no shrub of the field had yet grown on the land, and no plant of the field had yet sprouted, for the LORD God had not made it rain on the land, and there was no man to work the ground. [6] But mist would come up from the earth and water all the ground. [7] Then the LORD God formed the man out of the dust from the ground and breathed the breath of life into his nostrils, and the man became a living being.

MAN BECOMES A LIVING BEING

Nature is not just man's playground—it is also our background. Although we are meant to care for God's creation, we are not to lose sight of the fact that we are made from this very creation. God's world contained the ingredients with which God made the first human being.

The profound relationship is demonstrated in two specific ways. First, God personally formed man's physical body, which tells us a lot about how we can view our bodies and others' bodies. We are not to worship our bodies and expect them to be far more for us than they can be, but we shouldn't be indifferent to our bodies, treating them as if they have no special meaning or purpose. Instead, we must worship God *with* our bodies, and use them for the purposes He made them for.

Second, man was specially created by God breathing His own breath into him. God took the raw materials of creation—the dust of the ground—and breathed life into man. The air we breathe is drawn with a divine breath. Such truth adds a sense of wonder to what we understand to be true about our biology and our atmosphere. There is more to our existence than what science can explain. When we see the natural world and the wonders that human beings are, and as we draw each breath, we should reflect praise back to God.

This fusion of earth and breath reinforces for us that we completely rely on God for life, start to finish. Should God withdraw our breath, we return to the dust from which we are made. Our lives are never our own. This truth is as stunning as it is humbling.

Nature is not just man's playground—
it is also our background.

REFLECTIONS

Given that we are made of the earth, what should our posture be toward other forms of life on this planet we share?

How does the fact that God made your body influence what you do with your body?

Life is fragile, temporary, and a gift. How does this affect the way we live it?

INSIGHT

The word for man in Hebrew (the language of Genesis) is similar to the word for ground. As is the word life and living. From the very beginning human beings were to stand between God and His creation and rule in His stead. Part of what it means to be made in the image of God is to be a steward of what God owns. As we came from the ground that God made, we tend the ground until we are returned to the ground.

GENESIS 2:8-9

[8] The Lord God planted a garden in Eden, in the east, and there he placed the man he had formed. [9] The Lord God caused to grow out of the ground every tree pleasing in appearance and good for food, including the tree of life in the middle of the garden, as well as the tree of the knowledge of good and evil.

<table>
<tr><td>DAY
9</td><td></td></tr>
</table>

A GARDEN IN EDEN

The relationship between humans and the rest of creation does not end with formation and breath. The earth is also God's chosen means for providing the sustenance we need to fuel our mandate to practice dominion. A perfect environment was created to sustain and nurture human life.

The garden is described primarily as the ideal place for providing food for humans. The sources of water fuel the instruments of provision. The garden's very name reflects the water source that made such a perfect place possible for humankind to dwell. Eden's headwaters were mighty and were the primary contributor to the sacredness of this bountiful garden. The Creator stocked the garden with everything that His special human creation would need in accordance with His design.

There has never been a time when we have not depended on God for our existence. There has never been a time when God's provision for us has not been directly related to the earth. Our relationship with the earth is an interdependent one by God's design. Humans are in no position to use their dominion over God's creation as a reason for conquering or abusing God's creation. God has designed the world in such a way that the earth needs humans to care for it, and the humans are called to care for the earth.

Beyond the physically blessing Eden provided, it was a place where God met with people and lived in uninterrupted fellowship with them. More than what it provided the first human beings materially, it provided for them spiritually. Eden met all of humankind's desires and needs in full.

The Creator stocked the garden with everything
that His special human creation would
need in accordance with His design.

REFLECTIONS

How does the relationship between God and man in Eden teach us about what it looks like to depend on God and receive care from Him?

Brainstorm a list of ways you can experience God's care for you through nature.

What actions can you take to help your community restore or improve its environment as a way to demonstrate your love for God, His care for you, and your thankfulness for His provision?

CONNECTING THE STORY.

Eden is a "thin place" where God met with people. Though this place of beauty and abundance would be ruined by sin in the coming chapters, Eden provides a pattern that was repeated in the tabernacle (Exodus 25–26), the temple, and was ultimately realized in Jesus Christ. Jesus is the true and better place where God meets with people.

Echoes of EDEN

One of the ways we become thoughtful readers of the Bible is by learning to recognize key themes and trace them through the whole of Scripture. Though the Bible is made of many stories, the Bible is truly telling one story—the story of how God created the world, sin distorted it, Jesus redeemed it, and God is recreating it.

The garden of Eden is primarily a place where God dwelled with His people. We find echoes of what we see in Eden throughout the Scriptures.

EDEN was the first place God dwelled with human beings.

> *The LORD God planted a garden in Eden, in the east, and there he placed the man he had formed.*
> **GENESIS 2:8**

The glory of God was in His presence as He met with Moses on **MOUNT SINAI**.

> *The glory of the LORD settled on Mount Sinai, and the cloud covered it for six days. On the seventh day he called to Moses from the cloud. The appearance of the LORD's glory to the Israelites was like a consuming fire on the mountaintop. Moses entered the cloud as he went up the mountain, and he remained on the mountain forty days and forty nights.*
> **EXODUS 24:16-18**

God instructed Moses to build a **TABERNACLE** where He would again be present with His people.

> The cloud covered the tent of meeting, and the glory of the LORD filled the tabernacle. Moses was unable to enter the tent of meeting because the cloud rested on it, and the glory of the LORD filled the tabernacle.
> **EXODUS 40:34-35**

Solomon built the **TEMPLE** to be a more permanent tabernacle where God would again be with His people.

> When the priests came out of the holy place, the cloud filled the LORD's temple, and because of the cloud, the priests were not able to continue ministering, for the glory of the LORD filled the temple.
> **1 KINGS 8:10–11**

JESUS is the fullness of the presence of God wrapped in human flesh.

> The Word became flesh and dwelt among us. We observed his glory, the glory as the one and only Son from the Father, full of grace and truth.
> **JOHN 1:14**

Eventually, God will bring a **NEW CREATION** where the perfection of Eden is restored.

> Then I heard a loud voice from the throne: Look, God's dwelling is with humanity, and he will live with them. They will be his peoples, and God himself will be with them and will be their God. He will wipe away every tear from their eyes. Death will be no more; grief, crying, and pain will be no more, because the previous things have passed away.
> **REVELATION 21:3–4**

GENESIS 2:10-17

[10] A river went out from Eden to water the garden. From there it divided and became the source of four rivers. [11] The name of the first is Pishon, which flows through the entire land of Havilah, where there is gold. [12] Gold from that land is pure; bdellium and onyx are also there. [13] The name of the second river is Gihon, which flows through the entire land of Cush. [14] The name of the third river is Tigris, which runs east of Assyria. And the fourth river is the Euphrates.

[15] The Lord God took the man and placed him in the garden of Eden to work it and watch over it. [16] And the Lord God commanded the man, "You are free to eat from any tree of the garden, [17] but you must not eat from the tree of the knowledge of good and evil, for on the day you eat from it, you will certainly die."

<table>
<tr><td>DAY
10</td><td># LOCATION IS
EVERYTHING</td></tr>
</table>

The three greatest words in real estate are: location, location, and location. When we used the word location this way, we aren't designating a specific geographical point on a map but emphasizing the strategic location of a home or business. Recognizing that a place is in a great location says nothing specific about where it is but says everything about how well placed it is in the community. What matters most is how well the location serves the purposes of the potential residents in the community. This is the gist behind the Bible's mention of the location of the garden of Eden. A general geographical location is implied but a specific latitude and longitude are not given. The writer's point wasn't giving us a location that could be found but communicating how God perfectly placed Eden for the benefit of those who lived there.

God placed the man in this ideal location and tasked him with caring for the sacred space God provided. The work God gave was not work for work's sake; rather, it was participation in creation. God brought order out of chaos, and here man joined God in that effort through his work in the garden.

Verses 8 and 9 two specific trees in the garden. The Tree of Life offered fruit that extended earthly life, and the Tree of Knowledge of Good and Evil, which would have provided a whole range of knowledge within the categories of good and evil. These trees are referenced again in verse 17. The Tree of Life was not forbidden, but the Tree of Knowledge of Good and Evil was. Eating from it would result in being doomed to die. The people were free in the garden, but freedom has no meaning if there are no restrictions.

The Tree of Knowledge of Good and Evil is meant to give human beings moral instruction and boundaries. Good is what aligns with what God says and evil is what departs from it. The first good the man and woman learned was that this tree was restricted. This was a good and wise boundary from God.

Eden was an ideal location where
God placed man and tasked him with
caring for the sacred space God provided.

REFLECTIONS

How does seeing your location as a community into which God has placed you change the way you see your roles and responsibilities there?

Consider your attitude toward your responsibilities and work. Do you see work as a means of participating in the divine work of creation? Why or why not?

What moral boundaries are you tempted to cross? What freedom is being promised by crossing them? How does crossing boundaries actually enslave you? How does keeping them actually free you?

GENESIS 2:18-20

[18] Then the LORD God said, "It is not good for the man to be alone. I will make a helper corresponding to him." [19] The LORD God formed out of the ground every wild animal and every bird of the sky, and brought each to the man to see what he would call it. And whatever the man called a living creature, that was its name. [20] The man gave names to all the livestock, to the birds of the sky, and to every wild animal; but for the man no helper was found corresponding to him.

SOMETHING IS NOT GOOD

Verse 18 begins with the phrase, "Then the LORD God said." These words are reminiscent of the many times in Genesis 1 where God spoke things into existence and declared them "good." Yet this time, something was "not good." Man's solitude was "not good." The writer didn't mention whether the man felt alone or agreed with this assessment. But God's words are truth. An elegant environment for noble work may sound ideal to some, but to the Lord, it was insufficient for His special creation.

God's solution was to provide a suitable helper. The word "helper" is worthy of attention, not only for the insights that it offers in and of itself, but also for the ways the phrase is misunderstood and misapplied today. Far from implying any sort of subservient status to the man, "helper" simply defines the role this created being would play in giving aid and support to the man who clearly needed it in his solitude. The same phrase was used to describe God in His support of Israel in battle, suggesting something divinely special about the role (Deuteronomy 33:29; Psalm 33:20; 70:5; 121:2; Hosea 13:9).

To drive the point home, God gave the man a task of naming the animals in their kind, as if the exercise would help him realize no other creature corresponded to him. None of the other beings created from the earth were suitable. Man needed something (or someone!) that an animal couldn't provide (as wonderful as animals are). The story up to this point sets the stage for something truly special about humanity and the male/female relationship that serves as the fabric of human society.

God gave the man a task of naming the animals in their kind, as if the exercise would help him realize no other creature corresponded to him.

REFLECTIONS

How important are social relationships to God? How important are they to you?

In what ways have you found human relationships to be more rewarding than interactions with other living beings?

What is the implication of identifying the woman as a "helper" for man?

GENESIS 2:21-25

[21] So the LORD God caused a deep sleep to come over the man, and he slept. God took one of his ribs and closed the flesh at that place. [22] Then the LORD God made the rib he had taken from the man into a woman and brought her to the man. [23] And the man said:

> This one, at last, is bone of my bone
>
> and flesh of my flesh;
>
> this one will be called "woman,"
>
> for she was taken from man.

[24] This is why a man leaves his father and mother and bonds with his wife, and they become one flesh. [25] Both the man and his wife were naked, yet felt no shame.

HELPER DEFINED

The different process by which God created the right helper for man further highlights just how special the helper was. God Himself cared for Adam, carved out from Adam, and created for Adam. That Adam was a contributor but not a spectator to the creation process only added to his joy when the helper was later revealed. What a special relationship humanity has with the Creator, and what a generous, loving God He is!

It's also significant that God escorted His new creation to Adam similarly to the way He brought the different animals to Adam earlier. Yet in this momentous occasion, Adam recognized that his new corresponding helper was as human as him. She (and the fact that God did this for him) was so astounding to Adam that he broke out into song. Adam had clearly spoken before in naming the animals, but his first recorded words in Scripture are a song about the helper God gave him. Her uniqueness resulted in a unique exclamation of joy and purpose.

The natural outcome of the initial union between the first couple was the formal establishment of their relationship, as their duty involved procreation and the stewardship of the earth (Genesis 1:28). The writer shows that God's charge to fill and subdue the earth is fulfilled. Familial commitments lead to more familial commitments and weave the fabric of society.

The chapter ends with the first human community being created. From the very beginning our lives have been designed to be devoted to God and devoted to others who bear His image.

Adam's first recorded words in Scripture are a song about the helper God gave him.

REFLECTIONS

Adam identified similarities and differences with his helper. In what ways are men and women very similar, and in what ways are they very different?

How does this passage speak to the conversations about sexuality and gender in our day?

Are marriage and family as valued and protected today as they should be? Why or why not?

CONNECTING THE STORY

Marriage and family are the basic building blocks of human society. Throughout the Bible God's relationship to His people is that of a groom to his bride. This is not explicitly stated in the Old Testament, but at many points God is described by His fidelity to His people (Deuteronomy 7:9; Psalms 119:90). In the New Testament, the church is the bride of Christ (Ephesians 5:21-24); and the whole Bible culminates at the marriage supper of the Lamb (Revelation 19:7-8).

PAUSE & LISTEN

Spend some time reflecting over the week's reading.

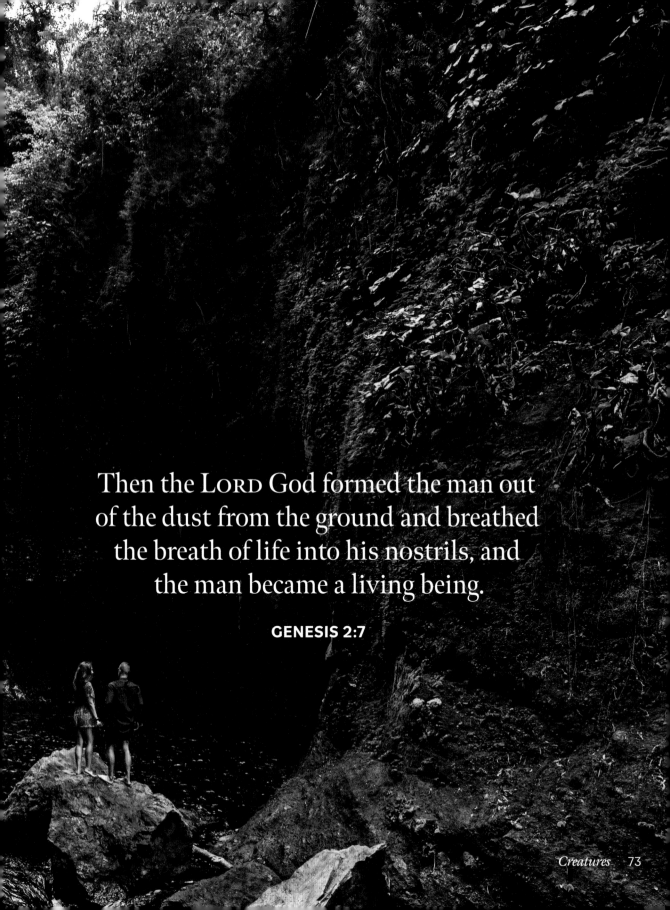

Then the LORD God formed the man out of the dust from the ground and breathed the breath of life into his nostrils, and the man became a living being.

GENESIS 2:7

REFLECTION

Use these questions for personal reflection or group discussion on Genesis 2:4-25.

What stuck out to you most in this week's reading? What surprised you? Confused you?

What does this week's Scripture teach you about God and His character?

What does this week's Scripture teach you about humanity and our need for grace?

What is one way the idea of being made in the image of God impacts the way we live?

What steps of faith and obedience is God asking you to take through these Scriptures?

PRAY

Gracious Father, thank You for creating us in Your image to be in relationship with You and each other. May we never lose sight of the value and dignity You have given all of us.

WEEK 3

CORRUPTION

The world is no longer all
that it was created to be.

Expectations are often nothing more than premeditated resentments. This is especially true when it comes to relationships and experiences that we have long been looking forward to.

A soon-to-be husband or wife may initially feel his or her spouse will solve all their problems, but it won't be long before both realize their marriage is not a solution for problems as much as it is a partnership for navigating them.

Or perhaps we give in to the powerful sales and marketing machines that promise perfect vacations, knowing full well the place or the experience can't be nearly as wonderful as promised. As a result, we expect quality family time and endless thrills, but end up with sore feet, sunburn, and long lines.

All of this is because our world has fallen. The world is no longer all that it was created to be, and we are not all that we were created to be. We are not merely victims of a broken world; we are primary contributors to the world's brokenness. The net results are broken experiences and relationships that taint us and everyone around us.

Genesis 3 is the story of how this brokenness came to be. Theologians call this event "the fall." Why are things the way they are? If you've read this many times before, do not allow your familiarity with the story to prevent you from taking a longer, harder look at the fall and its consequences. By looking deeper, you will also find God to be remarkably gracious and merciful in ways that might surpass your expectations.

GENESIS 3:1-7

THE TEMPTATION AND THE FALL

3 Now the serpent was the most cunning of all the wild animals that the Lᴏʀᴅ God had made. He said to the woman, "Did God really say, 'You can't eat from any tree in the garden'?"

² The woman said to the serpent, "We may eat the fruit from the trees in the garden. ³ But about the fruit of the tree in the middle of the garden, God said, 'You must not eat it or touch it, or you will die.'"

⁴ "No! You will certainly not die," the serpent said to the woman. ⁵ "In fact, God knows that when you eat it your eyes will be opened and you will be like God, knowing good and evil." ⁶ The woman saw that the tree was good for food and delightful to look at, and that it was desirable for obtaining wisdom. So she took some of its fruit and ate it; she also gave some to her husband, who was with her, and he ate it. ⁷ Then the eyes of both of them were opened, and they knew they were naked; so they sewed fig leaves together and made coverings for themselves.

MISSING THE MARK

Perhaps you've seen the videos of young children inside the office of a child psychologist, unknowingly being filmed to monitor their behavior. The children are handed a treat and are told that the treat is for them, but they are forbidden from consuming it just yet. Only when the instructor returns are they permitted to enjoy the item. Reactions vary from astonishing patience to willful and uncaring disobedience.

This is like what happened to Adam and the woman. In their custom-made garden, God had placed the Tree of Knowledge of Good and Evil. Like everything else in the garden, this tree was for them. However, they were forbidden from eating from it for a time. The knowledge the tree would give them would be theirs but not until God was ready for them to have it.

The Serpent used this gap in time to give Adam and the woman the sense that God was not keeping the knowledge *for* them but was keeping it *from* them. Therefore, eating its fruit would be "good." The Serpent did not tempt Adam and the woman to rebel against God's authority directly but invited them on a journey to gain wisdom and something "good" apart from what God had provided for them.

This same tactic failed with Jesus, though. In Matthew 4:1-11, when Satan offered Jesus all the kingdoms of the world in exchange for worship, there was nothing wrong with the "fruit" of Jesus ruling the world. It was, after all, His to rule. What mattered was how and when. Unlike Adam and the woman, Jesus obeyed the Father.

It is a gift to be able to recognize sin as sin—far too often, sin looks like obedience. The most effective and powerful temptations put something in front of us that can be interpreted as good. Yet the greatest gift is the complete obedience of Jesus on our behalf. This is the central message of Scripture that we find in the gospel.

It is a gift to be able to recognize sin as sin.

REFLECTIONS

Have you ever thought God was being unjust by not permitting something you desired, only to later realize it was for your well-being?

What personal examples do you have of how the temptation to sin promised more than what you experienced?

What lessons about guarding ourselves against temptation do we learn from this passage?

INSIGHT

Sin is any failure to conform to the moral law of God in acts (the things we do), attitudes (the things we think or believe), or nature (the way we are).[4] In Hebrew, the word literally means to miss the mark. Its the idea of being outside of God's best for our lives. Sin is always wrong because we have stepped over a good boundary God set for our good.

GENESIS 3:8-13

SIN'S CONSEQUENCES

[8] Then the man and his wife heard the sound of the LORD God walking in the garden at the time of the evening breeze, and they hid from the LORD God among the trees of the garden. [9] So the LORD God called out to the man and said to him, "Where are you?"

[10] And he said, "I heard you in the garden, and I was afraid because I was naked, so I hid."

[11] Then he asked, "Who told you that you were naked? Did you eat from the tree that I commanded you not to eat from?"

[12] The man replied, "The woman you gave to be with me — she gave me some fruit from the tree, and I ate."

[13] So the LORD God asked the woman, "What have you done?"

And the woman said, "The serpent deceived me, and I ate."

<table>
<tr><td>DAY
16</td><td></td></tr>
</table>

FEAR AND SHAME

The pair that once walked with God now ran from God. They ate of the Tree of Knowledge of Good and Evil to be like God, and then they became fearful of even being near Him. They went from eating of God's trees to hiding from God among them. Their childlike trust in God was replaced with fear and shame.

Yet Moses (the author of the story) goes out of his way to characterize God as more like a soft and kind Father rather than a harsh and enraged deity. God asked questions of Adam and the woman designed to help them consider their actions and arrive at the truthful conclusions on their own but in His presence.

Adam did not fully come clean. He admitted his shame, as evidenced by his hiding from God and wearing make-shift clothing, but he was equally quick to indict the woman and God. She who was once his perfect partner was now the perfect scapegoat, and clearly God was responsible for it all since He had given her to him. For her part, the woman shifted blame to the serpent. She truly was the victim of deception, but she was a willfully rebellious person.

Sin carries immense destructive power. Each one of us has transgressed and felt the resulting separation from God. Driven by fear and shame, we have attempted to evade God's presence or disregard Him, perhaps in the hope that He wouldn't perceive our disobedience or would eventually overlook it. Efforts to assign responsibility to others, akin to the actions of Adam and the woman, only deepen our feelings of isolation and guilt.

What can be done to restore our relationship with our Creator?

Childlike trust in God was replaced
with fear and shame.

REFLECTIONS

In what ways do we still try to hide ourselves from God and others when we sin? Why is it always better to be open and honest about it?

What are some ways we twist God's Word? How can we guard against taking away from or adding to His Word?

What are some of the things we do to not feel the weight or results of our sin?

DEATH
in Adam.

LIFE
in Jesus.

Adam's sin plunged all of humanity into sin. Sin is now a part of our nature. To be human is to both be made in the image of God and corrupted by sin. That was true of all people until Jesus.

The New Testament presents Jesus a second or final Adam who succeeded where the first Adam did not. He was tested and passed (Matthew 4:1-11). Just as sin entered the world through one man, salvation and forgiveness has come from another. Paul works out this thought in Romans 5.

[12] Therefore, just as sin entered the world through one man, and death through sin, in this way death spread to all people, because all sinned. [13] In fact, sin was in the world before the law, but sin is not charged to a person's account when there is no law. [14] Nevertheless, death reigned from Adam to Moses, even over those who did not sin in the likeness of Adam's transgression. He is a type of the Coming One.

[15] But the gift is not like the trespass. For if by the one man's trespass the many died, how much more have the grace of God and the gift which comes through the grace of the one man Jesus Christ overflowed to the many. [16] And the gift is not like the one man's sin, because from one sin came the judgment, resulting in condemnation, but from many trespasses came the gift, resulting in justification. [17] If by the one man's trespass, death reigned through that one man, how much more will those who receive the overflow of grace and the gift of righteousness reign in life through the one man, Jesus Christ.

[18] So then, as through one trespass there is condemnation for everyone, so also through one righteous act there is justification leading to life for everyone. [19] For just as through one man's disobedience the many were made sinners, so also through the one man's obedience the many will be made righteous. [20] The law came along to multiply the trespass. But where sin multiplied, grace multiplied even more [21] so that, just as sin reigned in death, so also grace will reign through righteousness, resulting in eternal life through Jesus Christ our Lord.

ROMANS 5:12-21

Jesus succeeded where Adam failed.

He took our place on the cross as a sacrifice for sin. Everyone who places their faith in Jesus will leave their condemnation and shame from the first Adam behind and find glory and salvation in the Second Adam.

GENESIS 3:14-19

[14] So the Lord God said to the serpent:

Because you have done this,

you are cursed more than any livestock

and more than any wild animal.

You will move on your belly

and eat dust all the days of your life.

[15] I will put hostility between you and the woman,

and between your offspring

and her offspring.

He will strike your head,

and you will strike his heel.

[16] He said to the woman:

I will intensify your labor pains;

you will bear children with painful effort.

Your desire will be for your husband,

yet he will rule over you.

[17] And he said to the man, "Because you listened to your wife and ate from the tree

about which I commanded you, 'Do not eat from it':

The ground is cursed because of you.

You will eat from it by means of painful labor

all the days of your life.

[18] It will produce thorns and thistles for you,

and you will eat the plants of the field.

[19] You will eat bread by the sweat of your brow

until you return to the ground,

since you were taken from it.

For you are dust,

and you will return to dust."

CURSED

In His kindness, God approached His people and began reestablishing the relationship that they broke. We should not interpret God's kindness in approaching Adam and the woman to mean He is indifferent to sin. The Serpent, Adam, and the woman each faced consequences. Yet in each of their curses we see clear messages of hope and grace.

The Serpent, initially described as "crafty," was cursed because of his deception. He was destined to crawl on his belly and eat dust, both of which convey a life of humiliation and strife. But there was more to this curse than those things: destruction, at the heels of the woman's offspring, would be the serpent's ultimate end. He sought to best both God and man, yet he would be bested by both.

The woman also faced ramifications, though she was not said to be cursed. In her divinely given roles as helper and child bearer, the woman would experience the consequences of her sin. She would have an increased level of pain in bearing children and increased hostility in her relationship with her husband. That there would be great pain and suffering with two of life's greatest moments—marriage and childbirth—is one of the more heartbreaking aspects of the fall.

For his part, Adam would suffer not only in the relationship with his wife, made from his flesh, but also with the ground he was made from and cared for. He would labor and toil and gain far more useless return where he used to care and nurture and receive joy and life. Virtually every day of his now shortened life, Adam would feel the weight of his sin.

But hope and grace persist. The woman would still be the one to bring the promised child, who would crush the head of the Serpent, into the world. Who that would be was not yet revealed, yet we now know the decisive blow was struck by the perfect offspring of the woman, Jesus Christ, when He died on the cross.

But hope and grace persist.

REFLECTIONS

As you read the these curses and consequences of sin, list some ways you have experienced them personally.

How have you seen the consequences of sin be quite natural to the sin you or others have committed?

Why should we make every effort to avoid sin? What does this look like in your life?

GENESIS 3:20-24

[20] The man named his wife Eve because she was the mother of all the living. [21] The LORD God made clothing from skins for the man and his wife, and he clothed them.

[22] The LORD God said, "Since the man has become like one of us, knowing good and evil, he must not reach out, take from the tree of life, eat, and live forever." [23] So the LORD God sent him away from the garden of Eden to work the ground from which he was taken. [24] He drove the man out and stationed the cherubim and the flaming, whirling sword east of the garden of Eden to guard the way to the tree of life.

GRACE AFTER THE FALL

The grace of God remains front and center even when humankind's sin persists. The fact that Adam took time to name his partner (Eve) and that God provided animal skins as clothing for them suggests God would not leave or forsake them. That Adam named her as the mother of all the living also indicates that he believed God's promise to provide a new generation. Further, animals were slain to provide coverings for the couple that allowed them to be properly clothed in their service to God. God Himself made these sacrifices and garments, an act that alluded to the forthcoming sacrificial system given to Moses in the books that follow Genesis in the Bible and, ultimately, to the gift of Jesus.

Humankind did fall and would inevitably be tempted to get around their certain death by eating from the Tree of Life. So, they were expelled from the garden. Adam and Eve were forced to develop their own garden from cursed ground and face certain judgment from God's angels should they ever attempt to return to Eden.

It is a sad and dark irony. Adam and Eve got exactly what they wanted: to be like God in ways they were not yet like Him. Yet what they really needed was simply to be with God as creatures made in His image. The decision to be like God cost them being with God. The same is true for us today: At our core, we would rather be like God than enjoy being with Him.

The grace of God remains front and center
even when humankind's sin persists.

REFLECTIONS

In what ways are we tempted to be like God instead of enjoying God?

What are some ways you enjoy God regularly?

How is enjoying God and being thankful toward Him an act of faith and obedience?

CONNECTING THE STORY

Genesis 3:21 tells us God took skins and made clothes for Adam and Eve. God killed an animal that He made to cover Adam and Eve's shame, which was produced by their sin. This act looks forward to the lambs killed at the Passover (Exodus 12), the sacrificial system implemented in Leviticus (1:3–7), and the sacrificial work of Jesus on the cross (Hebrews 9:24).

GENESIS 4:1-16

CAIN MURDERS ABEL

4 The man was intimate with his wife Eve, and she conceived and gave birth to Cain. She said, "I have had a male child with the LORD's help." ² She also gave birth to his brother Abel. Now Abel became a shepherd of flocks, but Cain worked the ground. ³ In the course of time Cain presented some of the land's produce as an offering to the LORD. ⁴ And Abel also presented an offering — some of the firstborn of his flock and their fat portions. The LORD had regard for Abel and his offering, ⁵ but he did not have regard for Cain and his offering. Cain was furious, and he looked despondent.

⁶ Then the LORD said to Cain, "Why are you furious? And why do you look despondent? ⁷ If you do what is right, won't you be accepted? But if you do not do what is right, sin is crouching at the door. Its desire is for you, but you must rule over it."

⁸ Cain said to his brother Abel, "Let's go out to the field." And while they were in the field, Cain attacked his brother Abel and killed him.

⁹ Then the LORD said to Cain, "Where is your brother Abel?"

"I don't know," he replied. "Am I my brother's guardian?"

¹⁰ Then he said, "What have you done? Your brother's blood cries out to me from the ground! ¹¹ So now you are cursed, alienated from the ground that opened its mouth to receive your brother's blood you have shed. ¹² If you work the ground, it will never again give you its yield. You will be a restless wanderer on the earth."

¹³ But Cain answered the LORD, "My punishment is too great to bear! ¹⁴ Since you are banishing me today from the face of the earth, and I must hide from your presence and become a restless wanderer on the earth, whoever finds me will kill me."

¹⁵ Then the LORD replied to him, "In that case, whoever kills Cain will suffer vengeance seven times over." And he placed a mark on Cain so that whoever found him would not kill him. ¹⁶ Then Cain went out from the LORD's presence and lived in the land of Nod, east of Eden.

SIN ABOUNDS

The hostility among men promised in the wake of the fall in Genesis 3 immediately reared its ugly head in the story of Cain and Abel.

Precious little was said about much we might want to know in this passage. We don't know why Cain's sacrifice was unacceptable or why Abel's was acceptable. We are not told how or where God communicated. We learn nothing about how Cain lured Abel to his death, or how God marked Cain, or what that mark was. All of these gaps in the story work together to keep us focused on the point of the story, namely the effect of sin on human nature and our relationships, beginning with God.

Based on Cain's response to his rejected offering, we see that Cain clearly lacked a pure heart. He was angry with his brother, and he was angry with God. Sin was at work in the Cain's heart, and its ripple effect is shocking. Cain calculated his brother's death and executed it without remorse. When God approached Cain, like the way He had approached Adam and Eve, Cain's response was far worse than his father's had been. Adam admitted his crime, but Cain lied directly to God and tried to pardon himself of any responsibility. We can only imagine the impact this had on Adam and Eve, as they saw and felt firsthand the impact of the corruption they brought into the world.

While Adam and Eve were banned from God's presence, Cain was further banned from God's protection. Living as a hunter-gatherer would bring with it difficulties unknown to Cain and his relatives, including an increased risk of death. With this in view, Cain pleaded with God (in either selfishness or repentance), and God mercifully responded with a mark that gave Cain more protection than he deserved. The God who is just is also merciful.

The God who is just is also merciful.

REFLECTIONS

When have you seen sin have a more profound effect than what you might have expected?

How does Cain's story reflect ours?

How can we learn to accept what God says as good and right and love following and obeying Him?

INSIGHT

In Genesis 4:7, God describes sin as having a desire for Cain. This calls back to Genesis 3:16 and personifies sin as seeking an intimate relationship with us the same way a husband desires his wife. To combat this, like Cain needed to master his sin, we also to be master over our sin rather than letting it master us.

PAUSE & LISTEN

Spend some time reflecting over the week's reading.

I will put hostility between
you and the woman,
and between your offspring
and her offspring.
He will strike your head,
and you will strike his heel.

GENESIS 3:15

REFLECTION

Use these questions for personal reflection or group discussion on Genesis 3–4.

What stuck out to you most in this week's reading? What surprised you? Confused you?

What does this week's Scripture teach you about God and His character?

What does this week's Scripture teach you about humanity and our need for grace?

What does it mean to you to know that God made provision for our sin in Genesis 3:15?

What steps of faith and obedience is God asking you to take through these Scriptures?

WEEK 4

CATASTROPHE

Enter the flood.

The account of Noah and the flood takes our breath away, as it reveals that God is both just and the justifier. It is a heart-stopping demonstration of God's righteousness. He punishes sin, but He also graciously saves those who have faith in Him. In this way, the story of Noah and the flood points us to Jesus. The flood did not change the sinful human heart, but it did bring justice and graciously rescue a chosen lineage. Something more powerful and even more gracious would be required to change a human's heart. As Paul stated in Romans 3:26, "God presented (Jesus) to demonstrate his righteousness ... so that he would be just and justify the one who has faith in Jesus."

GENESIS 6:5-12

JUDGMENT DECREED

[5] When the LORD saw that human wickedness was widespread on the earth and that every inclination of the human mind was nothing but evil all the time, [6] the LORD regretted that he had made man on the earth, and he was deeply grieved. [7] Then the LORD said, "I will wipe mankind, whom I created, off the face of the earth, together with the animals, creatures that crawl, and birds of the sky — for I regret that I made them." [8] Noah, however, found favor with the LORD.

GOD WARNS NOAH

[9] These are the family records of Noah. Noah was a righteous man, blameless among his contemporaries; Noah walked with God. [10] And Noah fathered three sons: Shem, Ham, and Japheth.

[11] Now the earth was corrupt in God's sight, and the earth was filled with wickedness. [12] God saw how corrupt the earth was, for every creature had corrupted its way on the earth.

THE PROBLEM

The contrast between Genesis 1:31 and 6:5 could not be more stark. "God saw all that he had made, and it was very good indeed" had become something quite different: "The LORD saw that human wickedness was widespread on the earth and that every inclination of the human mind was nothing but evil all the time." In Genesis 1 and 2, God gave the land to His creatures. In Genesis 6 and following, He takes it from them.

Though the coming flood would certainly be an act of righteous judgment, God was not portrayed as being particularly angry leading up to the event. Rather, the Bible describes God as one who "grieves" over sin and its impact on humankind. God did not regret making humans; He regretted what humans had made of themselves in their sin, and God would settle the account. Through humankind's destruction, God would salvage them.

To that end, one man caught God's eye through his righteous conduct and character: Noah. Noah's fear of God and blameless life did not cause God to choose him. Noah was by no means sinless, and God is by no means required to show mercy to anyone. Noah clearly believed (that is, walked in) what he knew to be true about God, and that faith was counted to him as righteousness. As the author of Hebrews puts it, "By faith Noah, after he was warned about what was not yet seen and motivated by godly fear, built an ark to deliver his family. By faith he condemned the world and became an heir of the righteousness that comes by faith" (Hebrews 11:7).

God did not regret making humans; He regretted what humans had made of themselves.

REFLECTIONS

Why might things have been worse in Noah's day than they are in our day?
What advantages in grace do we have that they did not have?

How might understanding sin and judgment give us a better grasp on God's grace toward us?

Think about the lives of great Christians you know. What distinguishes their relationships with God?

CONNECTING THE STORY

In Genesis 6:6 when God "regretted" making human beings, this does not mean God wished He had some something differently. God is not limited as we are. He does not change and does not make decisions that He would regret. Rather, this means God was hurt by what His creation had made of itself. Similar language is used a few other places in the Old Testament (1 Samuel 15; Jonah 3:10).

GENESIS 6:13-22

¹³ Then God said to Noah, "I have decided to put an end to every creature, for the earth is filled with wickedness because of them; therefore I am going to destroy them along with the earth.

¹⁴ "Make yourself an ark of gopher wood. Make rooms in the ark, and cover it with pitch inside and outside. ¹⁵ This is how you are to make it: The ark will be 450 feet long, 75 feet wide, and 45 feet high. ¹⁶ You are to make a roof, finishing the sides of the ark to within eighteen inches of the roof. You are to put a door in the side of the ark. Make it with lower, middle, and upper decks.

¹⁷ "Understand that I am bringing a flood — floodwaters on the earth to destroy every creature under heaven with the breath of life in it. Everything on earth will perish. ¹⁸ But I will establish my covenant with you, and you will enter the ark with your sons, your wife, and your sons' wives. ¹⁹ You are also to bring into the ark two of all the living creatures, male and female, to keep them alive with you. ²⁰ Two of everything — from the birds according to their kinds, from the livestock according to their kinds, and from the animals that crawl on the ground according to their kinds — will come to you so that you can keep them alive. ²¹ Take with you every kind of food that is eaten; gather it as food for you and for them." ²² And Noah did this. He did everything that God had commanded him.

THE PLAN

Any good plan answers the following questions: who, what, when, where, why, and how. God's plan for the destruction of the earth and the preservation of Noah's family alongside some creatures answers all of these questions in summary fashion.

First, there is the ark. Its massive size (some 450 feet long) and significant displacement is awe-inspiring, but the fact that no sail or rudder was mentioned infers that while the ark provided safety, those inside were in God's hands. Second, there are its passengers. Noah and his family would represent humanity, but animals would also tag along. By including male and female of every living creature, God demonstrated His commitment to His promise in creation even though sin had wreaked havoc on the earth. In the same way that God brought the animals to Adam to be named, God would bring the animals to Noah to be saved.

As impressive as these elements are, Noah's faith shines brighter. Consider how deeply Noah had to trust God to be willing to do something that lacked common sense and had no precedent. Noah had to believe God when He said, in effect, "The very means by which I will destroy this world is the means by which you will be saved." Noah had to believe in life through death, and in this way, Noah's faith points to the life and death of Jesus. The very means by which God judged sin once and for all was the very means by which He brought life for all who believe.

Noah's faith points to the life and death of Jesus.

REFLECTIONS

Imagine you were in Noah's position. What questions might you have had for God?

How does a relationship with God lead to trust and obedience? Similarly, how do obedience and trust lead to a relationship with God?

How does God requiring us to believe in the life, death, and resurrection of Jesus for eternal salvation compare and contrast with God requiring Noah to build an ark for his temporary salvation?

CORRUPTION SPREADS, *but* A REMNANT REMAINS.

There are countless reasons we might investigate our ancestry. Doing so allows us to preserve and document our family's history for future generations. It's a way to pass down stories, traditions, and knowledge about our ancestors; it can help us better understand our cultural and ethnic heritage; and it can also facilitate connections with living relatives we may have lost touch with or were unaware of, cultivating a sense of belonging and connection. Discovering our family's history and the paths our ancestors took can help develop a stronger sense of personal identity and belonging too.

Perhaps these and other reasons played a part in the genealogies of Cain and Seth in Genesis 4 and 5. Yet by tracing these two genealogies, we get a sense of how progress relates to sin. Though there are many technological advances associated with every passing generation, the effects of sin advance with it. Progress in the areas of architecture, construction, and the arts do not overcome the effects of sin in the heart of mankind. Nothing humans can do can compensate for what they have done. It is only the common grace of God that keeps things from getting any worse than they are.

And things did continue to get worse. So much so that God decided to start over with the genealogical line of Seth, a line of people who, by His grace, genuinely walked with the Lord. From this line, we meet Noah, who will be a central figure in the book of Genesis and a righteous man through whom God was pleased to work.

GENESIS 7:1-10

ENTERING THE ARK

7 Then the Lᴏʀᴅ said to Noah, "Enter the ark, you and all your household, for I have seen that you alone are righteous before me in this generation. ² You are to take with you seven pairs, a male and its female, of all the clean animals, and two of the animals that are not clean, a male and its female, ³ and seven pairs, male and female, of the birds of the sky — in order to keep offspring alive throughout the earth. ⁴ Seven days from now I will make it rain on the earth forty days and forty nights, and every living thing I have made I will wipe off the face of the earth." ⁵ And Noah did everything that the Lᴏʀᴅ commanded him.

⁶ Noah was six hundred years old when the flood came and water covered the earth. ⁷ So Noah, his sons, his wife, and his sons' wives entered the ark because of the floodwaters. ⁸ From the animals that are clean, and from the animals that are not clean, and from the birds and every creature that crawls on the ground, ⁹ two of each, male and female, came to Noah and entered the ark, just as God had commanded him. ¹⁰ Seven days later the floodwaters came on the earth.

DAY 24

THE TRUST

God's sovereignty and Noah's willing obedience are on full display in today's passage. God spoke and Noah obeyed.

Yet again, God made note of Noah's character. While not sinless, he was righteous, and did not go unnoticed by God. Noah's goodness did not earn him salvation, but God did draw a clear distinction between Noah and those who would die in the flood. That Noah fully obeyed God prior to the beginning of the flood is only further evidence of Noah's outstanding character. That the flood begins when God said it would is further evidence of His sovereignty over the world He made. Verse 10 emphasizes that the rains fell precisely on the day God said they would in verse 4.

Though we may be tempted to make God's sovereignty and man's responsibility incompatible enemies, the Bible goes above and beyond to portray them as intimate friends. God's sovereignty does not overtake our role in making choices, and our choices do not override or negate God's sovereignty. Noah's story is an early example among many whereby we learn to trust in God and see the dynamic of His sovereignty and our choices at work.

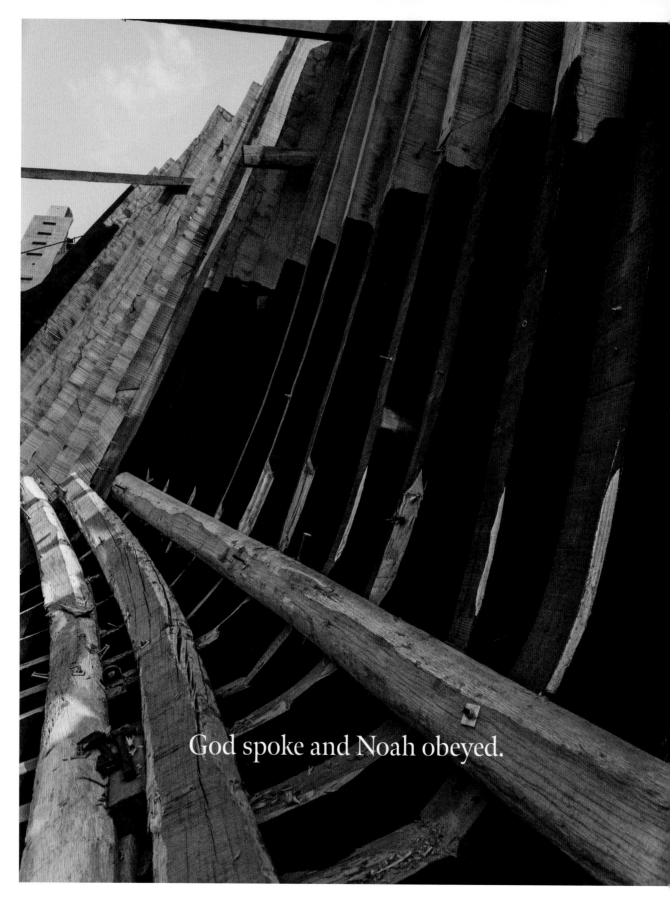

God spoke and Noah obeyed.

REFLECTIONS

How do you think God's sovereignty affects the way we make decisions? What happens to our decision-making ability if we have a misshapen view of God's sovereignty?

Why should God's sovereignty humble us when we think about our life situation? Why should God's sovereignty cultivate hope and trust?

Recall a time in your life when you doubted God's control but later realized how He had been working in your life all along.

GENESIS 7:11-16

THE FLOOD

[11] In the six hundredth year of Noah's life, in the second month, on the seventeenth day of the month, on that day all the sources of the vast watery depths burst open, the floodgates of the sky were opened, [12] and the rain fell on the earth forty days and forty nights. [13] On that same day Noah and his three sons, Shem, Ham, and Japheth, entered the ark, along with Noah's wife and his three sons' wives. [14] They entered it with all the wildlife according to their kinds, all livestock according to their kinds, all the creatures that crawl on the earth according to their kinds, every flying creature — all the birds and every winged creature — according to their kinds. [15] Two of every creature that has the breath of life in it came to Noah and entered the ark. [16] Those that entered, male and female of every creature, entered just as God had commanded him. Then the Lord shut him in.

<table>
<tr><td>DAY
25</td><td># THE FLOOD</td></tr>
</table>

The most significant decisions we make are marked by the date they happened. We know our birthdays. We know our wedding anniversaries. We know the dates when loved ones passed away. The flood is one of those moments in history marked with the same kind of importance in today's passage. Verses 11-12 state, "In the six hundredth year of Noah's life, in the second month, on the seventeenth day of the month, on that day all the sources of the vast watery depths burst open, the floodgates of the sky were opened, and the rain fell on the earth forty days and forty nights." There can be no doubting the author's intent to designate the flood account as real history. While we may not be able to specifically date the event according to our calendars, the biblical writer clearly wants us to know the flood occurred at a specific point in history.

The writer also wants his readers to know that just as the flood occurred as God said it would, God cared and provided for those He said He would. God Himself is said to have closed the door to the ark. It was His divinely-provided protection that kept Noah and other beings safe from God's judgment. Noah did his part and God did His.

Yet one cannot help but wonder what life was like for those not in the ark as the rains fell. Jesus gives us this answer in Matthew 24:38-39: "For in those days before the flood they were eating and drinking, marrying and giving in marriage, until the day Noah boarded the ark. They didn't know until the flood came and swept them all away." In the same way that the flood caught all but Noah and his family by surprise, the coming of Jesus will completely disrupt people going about their everyday lives. May we be ready as Noah!

Just as the flood occurred as God said it would,
God cared and provided for those He said He would.

REFLECTIONS

What are some significant dates that mark God's work in your life?

Is it possible to prepare for and celebrate an event if you don't know when it will occur? How can we be prepared for Christ's return?

How does anticipating the second coming of Christ increase our motivation for spreading the gospel?

GENESIS 7:17-24

[17] The flood continued for forty days on the earth; the water increased and lifted up the ark so that it rose above the earth. [18] The water surged and increased greatly on the earth, and the ark floated on the surface of the water. [19] Then the water surged even higher on the earth, and all the high mountains under the whole sky were covered. [20] The mountains were covered as the water surged above them more than twenty feet. [21] Every creature perished — those that crawl on the earth, birds, livestock, wildlife, and those that swarm on the earth, as well as all mankind. [22] Everything with the breath of the spirit of life in its nostrils — everything on dry land died. [23] He wiped out every living thing that was on the face of the earth, from mankind to livestock, to creatures that crawl, to the birds of the sky, and they were wiped off the earth. Only Noah was left, and those that were with him in the ark. [24] And the water surged on the earth 150 days.

THE DEVASTATION

Whereas Genesis 7:11-16 highlights God's saving work, today's passage highlights God's destructive work. The pervasiveness of humanity's sin was met with the pervasiveness of God's judgment through ever-rising waters that covered even the mountains. In Genesis 1, God's Spirit brought the chaos of the waters under His control for humanity's good. Now His Spirit released those waters in humankind's judgment.

Should there be any question about the extent of God's judgment, the words "all" or "every" are used eight times in as many verses. Everything Noah and his family knew to be their habitat was swallowed up in the great flood. Nothing—absolutely nothing—survived, except those in the ark.

The flood story highlights how God has the responsibility of caring for all that He has created. The sin that damaged His creation would not be allowed to fester. To be responsible for something is to respond on behalf of that something, and God responded in a way that left no doubt in anyone's mind as to who is in charge of this world.

While we may struggle to grasp the character of a God who would go to such lengths to demonstrate His righteousness, we need look no further than the sending of Jesus to see just how God's holiness and love converge in one great act of judgment and love. In His crucifixion, Jesus simultaneously took God's judgment and rescued those with faith in Him.

Jesus simultaneously took God's judgment
and rescued those with faith in Him.

REFLECTIONS

Why is it necessary for God to be both loving and holy?

When you consider the flood account, do you identify with Noah and his family or with those left outside the ark? Why?

The story of Noah, the ark, and the flood point to Jesus in many ways, some of which have been brought out already. In what other ways do you see Jesus in this story?

PAUSE & LISTEN

Spend some time reflecting over the week's reading.

Noah, however, found favor
with the LORD.

GENESIS 6:8

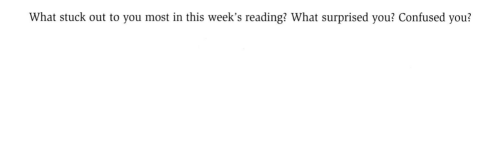

DAY
28

REFLECTION

Use these questions for personal reflection or group discussion on Genesis 6–7.

What stuck out to you most in this week's reading? What surprised you? Confused you?

What does this week's Scripture teach you about God and His character?

What does this week's Scripture teach you about humanity and our need for grace?

What are some ways that you see sin multiplying in our day?

What steps of faith and obedience is God asking you to take through these Scriptures?

WEEK 5

COVENANT

In all of it, God was just,
gracious, merciful, and true.

As the waters rose for some 150 days (Genesis 7:24), it's unlikely that Noah and his family questioned God's existence. They experienced exactly what He said they would and were spared the far worse fate all others faced. Perhaps they heard the screams of those clinging to the mountain tops as the waters rose as well as the eerie silence accompanied by creaking wood and falling rain. In all of it, God was just, gracious, merciful, and true.

Yet knowledge of such a God can still be tested by one of this world's most powerful resources: time. One can only imagine the mental anguish and the spiritual battles that roared within Noah and every member of his family inside the damp, dark ark. Even knowing and experiencing God can turn into doubting and hating God when we have to wait ... and wait ... and wait.

Eventually, wind replaced water, and rising turned into receding, all because "God remembered Noah, as well as all the wildlife and all the livestock that were with him in the ark" (Genesis 8:1). The promise to keep them was made and kept, though it was certainly tested by time.

To reflect on life in the ark is to reflect on life in the meantime—the time between a promise made and a promise kept. What is life supposed to look like while we wait for what we know it will one day look like?

It is, quite literally, a life of faith—faith in a God who always keeps His promises.

GENESIS 8:1-4

[1]God remembered Noah, as well as all the wildlife and all the livestock that were with him in the ark. God caused a wind to pass over the earth, and the water began to subside. [2] The sources of the watery depths and the floodgates of the sky were closed, and the rain from the sky stopped. [3] The water steadily receded from the earth, and by the end of 150 days the water had decreased significantly. [4] The ark came to rest in the seventh month, on the seventeenth day of the month, on the mountains of Ararat.

GOD REMEMBERED NOAH

We can scarcely imagine the trauma Noah and his family experienced in the ark. Incessant rain for a few hours can alter one's mood. Rain for 150 days that led to the destruction of all things and all life would have surely brought on an intense despair. Yes, they were safe and provided for, but to what end? No one would blame Noah and his family if they gave in to despair and cursed God for what they were experiencing.

Yet 150 days into the flood, we are told that "God remembered Noah, as well as all the wildlife and all the livestock that were with him in the ark." It was not as if the flood was God's means of "forgetting" or "trying to forget" humanity, and that suddenly God "remembered" a promise He had made. Rather, the expression means God acted in accordance with His earlier promises. The result of this "remembering" was to begin the process of removing all of the water from the earth. Yes, God was grieved when humanity corrupted His creation, but God's grief did not lead Him to forsake His promises to Adam and Eve in Genesis 3 or to Noah in Genesis 6.

God is a faithful God. Just as God is not indifferent to sin, God is equally committed to His promise to deliver His people from the injustice and violence in this world. He promotes goodness, eliminates harm, and remains engaged to provide healing. God's handling of evil may be gradual, yet His trustworthiness remains steadfast.

God's grief did not lead Him to forsake
His promises to Adam and Eve.

REFLECTIONS

Do you find it easier to seek and trust God when your life is challenging or when your life is easy? Reflect on why this is the case.

What circumstances or experiences of yours have led you to question God's faithfulness? How did God show Himself to be faithful?

How does this passage speak to us in the moments when we may feel abandoned or forgotten?

INSIGHT
When the Bible says that God "remembered" that doesn't mean that Noah was absent from God's mind or that there was every a time where God wasn't considering Noah, rather each time the phrase is used, it indicates that God is about to work on someone's behalf. Other examples include His intervention in the lives of Lot (Genesis 19:29), Rachel (Genesis 30:22), and the Israelites in Egypt (Exodus 2:24).

GENESIS 8:5-14

[5] The water continued to recede until the tenth month; in the tenth month, on the first day of the month, the tops of the mountains were visible. [6] After forty days Noah opened the window of the ark that he had made, [7] and he sent out a raven. It went back and forth until the water had dried up from the earth. [8] Then he sent out a dove to see whether the water on the earth's surface had gone down, [9] but the dove found no resting place for its foot. It returned to him in the ark because water covered the surface of the whole earth. He reached out and brought it into the ark to himself. [10] So Noah waited seven more days and sent out the dove from the ark again. [11] When the dove came to him at evening, there was a plucked olive leaf in its beak. So Noah knew that the water on the earth's surface had gone down. [12] After he had waited another seven days, he sent out the dove, but it did not return to him again. [13] In the six hundred first year, in the first month, on the first day of the month, the water that had covered the earth was dried up. Then Noah removed the ark's cover and saw that the surface of the ground was drying. [14] By the twenty-seventh day of the second month, the earth was dry.

<table>
<tr><td>DAY
30</td><td># SIGNS OF LIFE</td></tr>
</table>

Humans have used birds in interesting ways throughout history. Trained carrier pigeons were used for centuries to carry small messages across great distances. Vikings would release a bird to soar above their ship. A bird that wouldn't leave the area of the ship indicated to them that land was not nearby, but a bird that flew away with purpose indicated land in that direction. As early as 1911, coal miners' regulations encouraged them to use canaries in mines to detect carbon monoxide and other toxic gases before they hurt humans. Canaries are far more sensitive to those gases than humans, so by carrying these birds with them, miners got an early indication of the presence of harmful gas.

Before all of these came Noah's use of birds to determine whether or not there was land available for habitation. Ravens are scavengers, living off garbage and carcasses—and there would have been plenty of those. In contrast, doves and pigeons cannot fly for very long in one outing, prefer lower elevations, and rely on vegetation for food.

That a dove retrieved an olive leaf told Noah just where things were in the earth's recovery and its ability to sustain life. That it was an olive leaf may have been especially significant to Noah and his family, possibly symbolizing the earliest fulfillment of God's promise of a new life. It was as if God was saying to them, "See? Everything really will begin anew and thrive."

We may experience many things in our lives that lead us to doubt God's faithfulness, but He never fails to keep His promises.

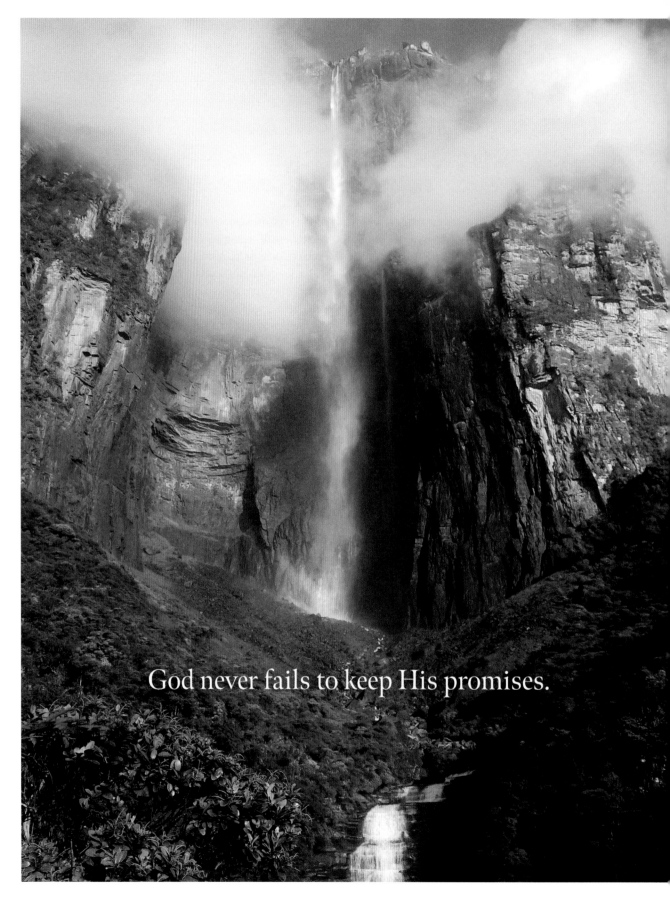

God never fails to keep His promises.

REFLECTIONS

If you had to choose between avoiding difficult times and not needing God and going through difficult times with God, which would you choose? Reflect on the consequences of your choice.

In this passage, God gave signs to Noah of the progress He was making in drying the earth. What signs has God given you that He is working in and through you?

How can you be certain that such "signs" are what you think they are? What role does Scripture play in helping you discern what God is up to?

COVENANT

A covenant is a chosen and binding relationship where two parties commit to support one another toward a goal. Covenants create a formal relationship with expectations for each side. The most common covenant in our culture today is marriage. Throughout the Bible there are five major covenants between people and God.

The Covenant with Noah

GENESIS 8:20–9:17. God made an unconditional promise to never again destroy the world through a flood like He did in the days of Noah. The rainbow was a sign of this covenant.

The Covenant with Abraham

GENESIS 12; 15; AND 17. God promised to bless Abraham with children, give his descendants a specific land on which to live (the promised land), and bless the whole world through Abraham's offspring. The sign for this covenant was circumcision.

The Covenant with Moses

EXODUS 19–24. After God rescued Israel from Egypt to make them a great nation and fulfill His promise to Abraham, He made a covenant with Moses and Israel by giving them a group of commandments to follow. The Israelites would find blessings if they obeyed and hardship if they disobeyed. The sign for this covenant was a day of rest (the Sabbath).

The Covenant with David

2 SAMUEL 7. God made a promise to David that a descendant from his line would rule forever over the house of Israel. God called Israel to be faithful but promised to fulfill the promise whether they were faithful or not. Unlike the other covenants, this one had no sign.

The New Covenant

JEREMIAH 31:31-34; EZEKIEL 36:22-32; LUKE 22:19-22. God made an unconditional promise to give people who follow Him a new heart by placing His Spirit inside of them. This covenant was promised by the prophets but fulfilled in Jesus. The sign for this covenant is the Lord's Supper which Christians celebrate together to remember Jesus's death and proclaim it until He returns.

GENESIS 8:15-22

¹⁵ Then God spoke to Noah, ¹⁶ "Come out of the ark, you, your wife, your sons, and your sons' wives with you. ¹⁷ Bring out all the living creatures that are with you—birds, livestock, those that crawl on the earth—and they will spread over the earth and be fruitful and multiply on the earth." ¹⁸ So Noah, along with his sons, his wife, and his sons' wives, came out. ¹⁹ All the animals, all the creatures that crawl, and all the flying creatures—everything that moves on the earth—came out of the ark by their families.

²⁰ Then Noah built an altar to the LORD. He took some of every kind of clean animal and every kind of clean bird and offered burnt offerings on the altar. ²¹ When the LORD smelled the pleasing aroma, he said to himself, "I will never again curse the ground because of human beings, even though the inclination of the human heart is evil from youth onward. And I will never again strike down every living thing as I have done.

²²   As long as the earth endures,

seedtime and harvest, cold and heat,

summer and winter, and day and night

will not cease."

WORSHIP

There is no mention of God saying anything to Noah or others on the ark during the flood. It was only when the flood waters entirely receded and the earth was ready to support life that God spoke to those on board. Those who had entered the ark and survived the destruction of the earth because of the mercy of God could exit the ark and begin life anew. What God had determined to destroy, He was now determined to fill with life.

This major act of salvation also led to a special act of worship. Because God saved—because God restored His fellowship with humanity and brought creation back to Himself—Noah worshiped through an offering of thanksgiving and atonement for sin, and it was pleasing to the Lord. Before the flood, the Lord said, "I will wipe mankind, whom I created, off the face of the earth, together with the animals, creatures that crawl, and birds of the sky—for I regret that I made them" (6:7). In light of Noah's worship after his salvation, the Lord says the exact opposite: "I will never again curse the ground because of human beings, even though the inclination of the human heart is evil from youth onward. And I will never again strike down every living thing as I have done" (8:21). As long as the earth is the earth, God will never again strike every living thing.

God's promise depends on His goodness and nothing else. And with it, the Lord gave Noah and his family confidence they could thrive in this "new" earth. What was true for Noah and his family is true for us today. We are called to exercise our dominion as stewards of a creation that groans along with us as we wait for Jesus to return and establish the new heaven and the new earth.

Those who had entered the ark and survived the destruction of the earth because of the mercy of God could exit the ark and begin life anew.

REFLECTIONS

How does reflecting on God's promises help us live out our commitment to Him today?

God's speaking to Noah was surely of great comfort. What verses of Scripture have been particularly meaningful to you lately? Why?

What grade would you give humanity today on our stewardship of life and creation? What grade would you give yourself?

GENESIS 9:1-7

GOD'S COVENANT WITH NOAH

9 God blessed Noah and his sons and said to them, "Be fruitful and multiply and fill the earth. ² The fear and terror of you will be in every living creature on the earth, every bird of the sky, every creature that crawls on the ground, and all the fish of the sea. They are placed under your authority. ³ Every creature that lives and moves will be food for you; as I gave the green plants, I have given you everything. ⁴ However, you must not eat meat with its lifeblood in it. ⁵ And I will require a penalty for your lifeblood; I will require it from any animal and from any human; if someone murders a fellow human, I will require that person's life.

⁶   Whoever sheds human blood,

by humans his blood will be shed,

for God made humans in his image.

⁷ But you, be fruitful and multiply; spread out over the earth and multiply on it."

GUARDRAILS

Perhaps you've heard the statement, "Laws exist for the people who are prone to break them." The statement is usually brought up in a conversation when a certain law or regulation comes to light and someone thinks, "Who would even think about doing what that law prohibits?" Such laws or restrictions are a sad testimony to the human condition.

This idea is present in Genesis 9. Though the flood was over and only "righteous" Noah and his family were to fill the earth, and though they were permitted to eat animal flesh as part of their diet, the Lord gave a law in verse 4 to guide their eating: "However, you must not eat meat with its lifeblood in it." Restricting the lifeblood meant forbidding the eating of an animal while alive. An animal's blood was representative of its life force.

What was true for animals was all the more true for human beings who are made in God's image. To take the life of a person is a direct offense to the God who made him or her. Verse 6 implies that the burden of carrying out such an accounting sits with humans who are also impacted by such death, but humans are not the ultimate offended party. The value of a human life is rooted in its being a creation of God in His image.

What kind of person would hunt and then eat an animal while it was still alive? What kind of person would take the life of another person? The need for such provisions reveals much about God's knowledge of the depravity of the human heart. Just because humans could eat animals did not mean they could not respect and care for the animals, domestic or otherwise. Simply because all of human life had been taken in the flood did not mean sin in the human heart had been dealt with. These laws would instruct humans in the righteousness required of them, but it would not have its intended effect.

God's law instructs us in the
righteousness required of us.

REFLECTIONS

What impact do laws have on an immoral society?

What is the relationship between law and grace?

How does the law of God point us to Jesus?

CONNECTING THE STORY

Genesis 9:1-7 contains an early law of God that predates the giving of the law in full to Moses at Mount Sinai in the book of Exodus. The first five books of the Bible are collectively known as the Torah or the Law because they introduce us to the law-giving God as well as the laws He gives to set healthy and needed boundaries for the people made in His image. For the Christian, Jesus came to fulfill the law (Matthew 5:17).

GENESIS 9:8-17

[8] Then God said to Noah and his sons with him, [9] "Understand that I am establishing my covenant with you and your descendants after you, [10] and with every living creature that is with you — birds, livestock, and all wildlife of the earth that are with you — all the animals of the earth that came out of the ark. [11] I establish my covenant with you that never again will every creature be wiped out by floodwaters; there will never again be a flood to destroy the earth."

[12] And God said, "This is the sign of the covenant I am making between me and you and every living creature with you, a covenant for all future generations: [13] I have placed my bow in the clouds, and it will be a sign of the covenant between me and the earth. [14] Whenever I form clouds over the earth and the bow appears in the clouds, [15] I will remember my covenant between me and you and all the living creatures: water will never again become a flood to destroy every creature. [16] The bow will be in the clouds, and I will look at it and remember the permanent covenant between God and all the living creatures on earth." [17] God said to Noah, "This is the sign of the covenant that I have established between me and every creature on earth."

THE SIGN

Symbols are powerful as they represent greater things, ideals, and values—but they don't last forever. Many of them have existed for centuries, and as cultures change, their meanings also change. For example, the heart symbol is the most recognized representation of romantic love and affection. However, its ancient symbolism has nothing to do with love. For example, in ancient Greece, the heart shape was used as a symbol for a plant that was used for seasoning, medicine, perfume, and even an early form of birth control. The ancient city of Cyrene, which became rich from trading this plant, even incorporated the heart symbol on its money.[5] These meanings are a far cry from communicating affection!

Something similar has happened to the rainbow. The simple and relatively frequent display of sunlight shining through rain had certainly occurred many times over prior to God showing one to Noah as a symbol of His promise to never again flood the earth, but the mundaneness of the phenomenon did not dilute the significance of the meaning the Lord attached to it. This natural spectacle that holds such a powerful message in the Christian faith has often meant something entirely different to other people in other religions and been used by people with other convictions to carry meaning that is even hostile to the meaning God ascribes to it.

None of this changes God's original intent with His promise to maintain a relationship with humanity. Every rainbow is a picture of the salvation that graciously put us into a covenant relationship with God. As storms retreated and sun shone through the last remnants of falling moisture to form a colorful bow, we are reminded that of God's gracious nature toward us.

Every rainbow reminds us of the salvation that graciously put us into a covenant relationship with God.

REFLECTIONS

How does the covenant between God and Noah, symbolized by the rainbow, demonstrate God's mercy and promise to never flood the earth again?

How does God's covenant with Noah point us to God's covenant with us in Christ?

What steps can you take to renew the commitments you've made to God?

PAUSE & LISTEN

Spend some time reflecting over the week's reading.

And God said, "This is the sign of the covenant I am making between me and you and every living creature with you, a covenant for all future generations: I have placed my bow in the clouds, and it will be a sign of the covenant between me and the earth."

GENESIS 9:12-13

REFLECTION

Use these questions for personal reflection or group discussion on Genesis 8–9.

What stuck out to you most in this week's reading? What surprised you? Confused you?

What does this week's Scripture teach you about God and His character?

What does this week's Scripture teach you about humanity and our need for grace?

How do covenants point us to the goodness of God?

What steps of faith and obedience is God asking you to take through these Scriptures?

PRAY

God thank You for entering into a covenant with us through the blood of Your Son Jesus who cleansed us from all sin and brings us from life to death. Thank You for saving us.

WEEK 6

CONFUSION

The flood did not wipe clean
the heart of any sinner.

"You would think that he would have learned his lesson."

These are the all too common words of parents who have recently disciplined their children in a relatively severe way, proportional to the sins that were committed. Yet no sooner is the discipline over than does the child do the same or worse.

Similarly, one might think that Noah and his family would have begun their new lives on the straight and narrow and that even their children and grandchildren would have followed suit—if only because of their memories of the world's destruction in the flood. Genesis 9–11 tells a different story. Noah and his descendants fared the same as Adam and his. The genealogies of Genesis 10 and 11, along with the stories and occasional historical notes interspersed among them, show us the many ways human beings continued to earn God's judgment. The flood wiped the earth clean of nearly all its sinners, but it did not wipe clean the heart of any sinner.

These remaining chapters of Genesis force us to reckon with the fact that we are, at our core, sinners in rebellion against the God who made us and are incapable of doing anything about it. As the Lord said through Jeremiah, "The heart is more deceitful than anything else, and incurable—who can understand it?" (Jeremiah 17:9).

When God washed away nearly all of the world's sinners, sinners went right back to work ignoring Him or attempting to replace Him. Since God promised not to wash sinners away again, then perhaps He would one day wash sin away. Even these stories of people earning God's judgment contain glimpses of hope that God would do just that.

GENESIS 9:18-29

PROPHECIES ABOUT NOAH'S FAMILY

[18] Noah's sons who came out of the ark were Shem, Ham, and Japheth. Ham was the father of Canaan. [19] These three were Noah's sons, and from them the whole earth was populated.

[20] Noah, as a man of the soil, began by planting a vineyard. [21] He drank some of the wine, became drunk, and uncovered himself inside his tent. [22] Ham, the father of Canaan, saw his father naked and told his two brothers outside. [23] Then Shem and Japheth took a cloak and placed it over both their shoulders, and walking backward, they covered their father's nakedness. Their faces were turned away, and they did not see their father naked.

[24] When Noah awoke from his drinking and learned what his youngest son had done to him, [25] he said:

> Canaan is cursed.
>
> He will be the lowest of slaves to his brothers.

[26] He also said:

> Blessed be the Lord, the God of Shem;
>
> Let Canaan be Shem's slave.
>
> [27] Let God extend Japheth;
>
> let Japheth dwell in the tents of Shem;
>
> let Canaan be Shem's slave.

[28] Now Noah lived 350 years after the flood. [29] So Noah's life lasted 950 years; then he died.

SHAME CONTINUES

While we must acknowledge that no one is perfect, we should also give credit where credit is due. The Bible is fascinating in this regard, for it simultaneously recognizes moral excellence and moral depravity in the same person without apology or compromise.

At the beginning of the flood story, the Bible states that "Noah was a righteous man, blameless among his contemporaries; Noah walked with God" (Genesis 6:9). In the New Testament Noah is called "a preacher of righteousness" (2 Peter 2:5). Yet not long after settling into a new life after the flood, Noah lost himself to drunkenness and shamed himself with his nakedness.

Noah's son, Ham, caught him in this condition, which—in and of itself—was not sinful. While short on details, the story implies that Ham delighted in the fact that his father was drunk and naked and spoke to his brothers about it with intent to bring more shame on his father. For a father to bring such shame on himself was wrong, but for a son to delight in it rather than cover it was particularly heinous in their culture. This act exposed the heart of one who did not honor his father and held contempt for God's order of creation.

Though the takeaways from this story are many, we must recognize that anyone can make a mess of his or her life and sin against God and man—and everyone makes a mess of his or her life by sinning against God and man. Only the grace and mercy of God can help any of us.

Only the grace and mercy of
God can help any of us.

REFLECTIONS

Given how inconsistent human beings are, how can you tell if the Bible is being descriptive or prescriptive when narrating someone's story?

What are some of the challenges associated with thinking highly of someone and also knowing things about them that break the heart of God?

What practices and safeguards can you put in place to "grow in the grace and knowledge of our Lord and Savior Jesus Christ" (2 Peter 3:18)?

GENESIS 11:1-2

THE TOWER OF BABYLON

¹ The whole earth had the same language and vocabulary. ² As people migrated

from the east, they found a valley in the land of Shinar and settled there.

SETTLE FOR LESS

Genesis chapters 10 and 11 focus on genealogies of nations and people groups. The author includes them to show the relationship between the story of Noah and the flood to the story of Abraham and all who come after him through the rest of the book of Genesis. The story of the Tower of Babel that makes up the first part of Genesis 11 is a more detailed explanation of the comments about Nimrod in Genesis 10:8-12.

As would be expected, the people spoke the same language, yet some migrated eastward. One could read this verse and conclude that the people were being obedient to the mandate to fill the earth, yet given the rest of the story, one is led to believe that these people moved eastward intentionally to do what they tried to do. Far from being obedient, the people rapidly deteriorated in their desire to honor and obey the Creator, so much so that moving "eastward" would become synonymous with disobedience and death throughout the book of Genesis.

Human beings have a long track record of drifting or even sprinting eastward—rejecting God's blessing in favor of some other perceived good that we create ourselves. Sometimes we choose something good instead of what is best, and other times we blatantly choose what we know is contrary to the will of God and simply don't care anymore. In every biblical account, the result is ruin. Our personal stories are the same. Only God can save us from ourselves.

Human beings have a long track record
of drifting or even sprinting eastward.

REFLECTIONS

How have you seen culture drift "eastward" during your lifetime?

Is there anything "new under the sun" (Ecclesiastes 1:9) when it comes to some of the ways our culture has moved from God? Explain.

What impact does having the Holy Spirit in one's life have on one's "eastward drift"?

BABEL
&
PENTECOST

Babel shows a world that had become unified and lost the purpose that God had given it. Unity came together with human sinfulness and ingenuity to build a tower to ascend to God—to take His power for our own. In response God confused the people's language so that they could not communicate.

This was reversed at Pentecost.

After Jesus was raised from the dead and ascended into heaven, the apostle Peter preached a sermon to a gathered crowd who had come to Jerusalem to celebrate the Jewish feast of Pentecost. People were from all over and yet, by the power of the Holy Spirit, all understood Peter in their native language.

What had been separated and confused at Babel was united and clarified at Pentecost.

Together

The whole earth had the same language and vocabulary.

GENESIS 11:1

Separated

"Come, let's go down there and confuse their language so that they will not understand one another's speech."

GENESIS 11:7

Together

When the day of Pentecost had arrived, they were all together in one place.

ACTS 2:1

United

Suddenly a sound like that of a violent rushing wind came from heaven, and it filled the whole house where they were staying. They saw tongues like flames of fire that separated and rested on each one of them. Then they were all filled with the Holy Spirit and began to speak in different tongues, as the Spirit enabled them.

Now there were Jews staying in Jerusalem, devout people from every nation under heaven. When this sound occurred, a crowd came together and was confused because each one heard them speaking in his own language. They were astounded and amazed, saying, "Look, aren't all these who are speaking Galileans? How is it that each of us can hear them in our own native language? Parthians, Medes, Elamites; those who live in Mesopotamia, in Judea and Cappadocia, Pontus and Asia, Phrygia and Pamphylia, Egypt and the parts of Libya near Cyrene; visitors from Rome (both Jews and converts), Cretans and Arabs—we hear them declaring the magnificent acts of God in our own tongues." They were all astounded and perplexed, saying to one another, "What does this mean?"

ACTS 2:2–12

GENESIS 11:3-4

³ They said to each other, "Come, let's make oven-fired bricks." (They used brick for stone and asphalt for mortar.) ⁴ And they said, "Come, let's build ourselves a city and a tower with its top in the sky. Let's make a name for ourselves; otherwise, we will be scattered throughout the earth."

DAY
38

BETTER TOGETHER?

While there are many stories in the Bible that vividly portray the heart of man, Genesis 11 is among the most powerful. There was a clear and compelling vision by some to disobey and rebel against the Lord. Rather than live their lives in a way that made much of their Creator, they sought to make a name for themselves by building what was almost certainly a religious shrine that worshiped nature or man. Rather than scatter across the earth as they were told, they sought to gather together and never scatter again. Independence from God that others looked up to and admired—that's what the city of Babel and its construction work was all about.

We are no different today. The very heart of man is committed to making a name for itself. Equally fascinating is that engineering, construction, and architecture remain the primary means by which men seek the glory of man that is only due to God. Ironically, we do so by trying to create with the very things and on the planet given to us by the Creator. Man's attempts at archaeological greatness, be it the pyramids in Egypt or the skyscrapers in Dubai, are impressive from the ground and noticeable from the air but invisible from the heavens. The same is true with our philosophies, ideas, and technological advancements, as well as our digital platforms. Try as we might to usurp God's glory, we never do, and we never will.

Babel was a clear and compelling vision to disobey and rebel against the Lord.

REFLECTIONS

Is it possible to desire fame and influence for oneself and still be a follower of Jesus? Why or why not?

Which of your experiences has exposed your pride for the weakness that it actually is?

How is pride the beginning point of other kinds of sin as well? How have you seen pride lead to greater and greater destruction, either in your own life or in the lives of those around you?

GENESIS 11:5-9

[5] Then the LORD came down to look over the city and the tower that the humans were building. [6] The LORD said, "If they have begun to do this as one people all having the same language, then nothing they plan to do will be impossible for them. [7] Come, let's go down there and confuse their language so that they will not understand one another's speech." [8] So from there the LORD scattered them throughout the earth, and they stopped building the city. [9] Therefore it is called Babylon, for there the LORD confused the language of the whole earth, and from there the LORD scattered them throughout the earth.

RECAPTURING EDEN

The story of the Tower of Babel is eerily similar to the story of Adam and Eve. God expelled Adam and Eve from the garden knowing full well what they would do themselves and against Him if they had access to the Tree of Life. Similarly, knowing completely the damage humankind would do to itself and against the Lord should they be allowed to stay in once place and exalt themselves, God confounded their language.

This preventative act of mercy positioned mankind to fulfill their command to scatter all over the earth, even though they would have preferred to gather. God is for us even when we are only for ourselves. And we should not miss the irony of this moment in history: people set out to make a name for themselves, but when God confused their language, the place was named for what God did to them.

From the very beginning of Genesis, God had a plan to bless human beings by providing everything good for them, yet human beings were (and are) quick to dismiss His goodness and try to grasp their version of good on their own. Rather than be fruitful and fill the good earth that God provided, men set out to leave it and create their own good. Our selfish ambition is seemingly inescapable. We keep getting in our own way. What can be done to rescue us from ourselves?

God had a plan to bless humans
by providing everything good for them,
yet human beings were quick to dismiss His
goodness and try to grasp their version of good.

REFLECTIONS

What life experiences have you had that you initially resented but later came to see that God was working for your good?

How do we benefit from acknowledging our limitations before God?

How does studying the big picture of God's unfolding story affect your view and understanding of your own?

GENESIS 11:10-32

FROM SHEM TO ABRAM

[10] These are the family records of Shem. Shem lived 100 years and fathered Arpach-shad two years after the flood. [11] After he fathered Arpachshad, Shem lived 500 years and fathered other sons and daughters. [12] Arpachshad lived 35 years and fathered Shelah. [13] After he fathered Shelah, Arpachshad lived 403 years and fathered other sons and daughters. [14] Shelah lived 30 years and fathered Eber. [15] After he fathered Eber, Shelah lived 403 years and fathered other sons and daughters. [16] Eber lived 34 years and fathered Peleg. [17] After he fathered Peleg, Eber lived 430 years and fathered other sons and daughters. [18] Peleg lived 30 years and fathered Reu. [19] After he fathered Reu, Peleg lived 209 years and fathered other sons and daughters. [20] Reu lived 32 years and fathered Serug. [21] After he fathered Serug, Reu lived 207 years and fathered other sons and daughters. [22] Serug lived 30 years and fathered Nahor. [23] After he fathered Nahor, Serug lived 200 years and fathered other sons and daughters. [24] Nahor lived 29 years and fathered Terah. [25] After he fathered Terah, Nahor lived 119 years and fathered other sons and daughters. [26] Terah lived 70 years and fathered Abram, Nahor, and Haran.

[27] These are the family records of Terah. Terah fathered Abram, Nahor, and Haran, and Haran fathered Lot. [28] Haran died in his native land, in Ur of the Chaldeans, during his father Terah's lifetime. [29] Abram and Nahor took wives: Abram's wife was named Sarai, and Nahor's wife was named Milcah. She was the daughter of Haran, the father of both Milcah and Iscah. [30] Sarai was unable to conceive; she did not have a child.

[31] Terah took his son Abram, his grandson Lot (Haran's son), and his daughter-in-law Sarai, his son Abram's wife, and they set out together from Ur of the Chaldeans to go to the land of Canaan. But when they came to Haran, they settled there. [32] Terah lived 205 years and died in Haran.

CONTINUED FAITHFULNESS

One of the more useful features found among online media players is the ability to play the video or audio at a higher rate of speed. Sometimes the information one is taking in is easily consumable and the more rapid playback saves time, but other times it's just a useful tool for advancing to "the good part" in a book or podcast that you know is coming.

In a sense, the genealogy that ends Genesis 11 does both. It's not as if the people of earth suddenly gained spiritual momentum after what happened at Babel. The ten generations listed from Shem to Terah almost assuredly represent a steady spiritual decline, though not without God saving a remnant of people who remained faithful to Him. In fact, this genealogy shows that God determined to deal with a select group of people as His own and to give the others over to their desires (Romans 1:24-28).

Perhaps this is also why verses 27-32 provide more detail about Abraham. The eight names listed are not a part of a genealogy but explain the relationships between all of the people we will read about in the many chapters to come. God's story grows increasingly focused as it unfolds.

The remainder of Genesis focuses on Abraham and his family. While they were not perfect men and women, they were faithful. Through them, we see God working in history and making a way to bless the whole world using this one family.

This man's family line will lead to Jesus Christ who Matthew calls: "Jesus Christ, the Son of David, the Son of Abraham" (Matthew 1:1).

God's story continues to unfold, and it is a pleasure to be among its characters and in His faithfulness.

As God's story continues to unfold, it's a pleasure to be among its characters and in His faithfulness.

REFLECTIONS

What kinds of responses do you think we would get if we asked a random sample of people in our city, "What is wrong with the world?"

Do you think of yourself as responsible for what is wrong with the world? Why or why not?

As mentioned above, genealogies have a way of not just looking back but also pointing forward to God's unfolding story. What promise of God do you most need in your life today? How does that promise give you hope?

CONNECTING THE STORY

When reading through the Bible, you may have the tendency to skip the genealogies—the family records of biblical characters who you are unfamiliar with and don't see how they advance the story. Each genealogy is a record of God's faithfulness to do what He said, to take broken people and broken families and share His goodness and grace in and through their lives. If you are tempted to skip, resist. Press in and see how God has been faithful in the past and believe He will be in the future.

PAUSE & LISTEN

Spend some time reflecting over the week's reading.

So from there the LORD scattered them throughout the earth, and they stopped building the city.

GENESIS 11:8

REFLECTION

Use these questions for personal reflection or group discussion on Genesis 10–11.

What stuck out to you most in this week's reading? What surprised you? Confused you?

What does this week's Scripture teach you about God and His character?

What does this week's Scripture teach you about humanity and our need for grace?

How does the gospel offer clarity to a world confused by sin?

What steps of faith and obedience is God asking you to take through these Scriptures?

PRAY

God thank You for Your faithfulness despite our sinfulness. Help us to choose
Your ways over our own ways.

PHOTOGRAPHY CREDITS

ENDNOTES

1. *Adapted from Robert D. Bergen, "Genesis," in CSB Study Bible: Notes, ed. Edwin A. Blum and Trevin Wax (Nashville, TN: Holman Bible Publishers, 2017), 1–3.*
2. *Taken from Bergen, 3.*
3. *"Apostles' Creed," The Gospel Coalition, accessed September 12, 2023, https://www.thegospelcoalition.org/publication-online/apostles-creed/.*
4. *Wayne A. Grudem, Systematic Theology: An Introduction to Biblical Doctrine (Leicester, England; Grand Rapids, MI: Inter-Varsity Press; Zondervan Pub. House, 2004), 1254.*
5. *Lindsay Gandolfo, "The Heart: A Love Story," Columbia Surgery, accessed November 1, 2023, https://columbiasurgery.org/news/heart-love-story#:~:text=Silphium%20–%20Legend%20of%20the%20Heart%2DShaped%20Plant&text=In%20the%206th%20century%20CE,early%20form%20of%20birth%20control.*

Step into God's beautiful story.

Storyteller is a Bible study series uniquely designed to be inviting, intuitive, and interactive. Each volume examines a key theme or story in a book of the Bible. Every week includes five days of short Scripture reading, a daily thought explaining each passage, a short list of questions for a group Bible study, and space for you to write down your discoveries. And new volumes are being added every year.

Learn more online or call 800.458.2772.
lifeway.com/storyteller

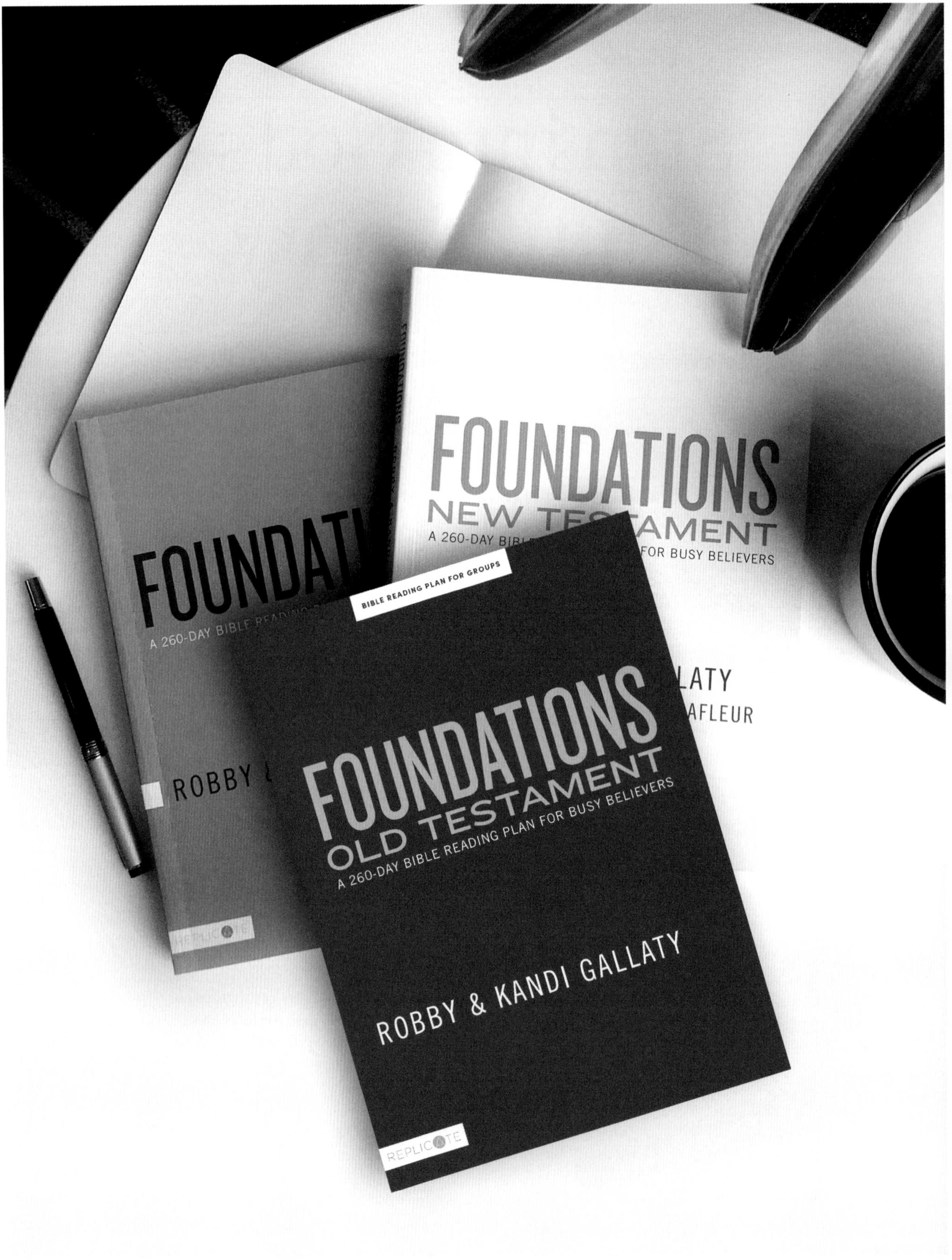
BIBLE READING PLAN FOR GROUPS
FOUNDATIONS
OLD TESTAMENT
A 260-DAY BIBLE READING PLAN FOR BUSY BELIEVERS
ROBBY & KANDI GALLATY
REPLICATE
FOUNDATIONS
NEW TESTAMENT

Manageable one-year plans for Bible reading

Foundations gives you a one-year Bible reading plan that requires just five days of study per week to fit your busy schedule. It includes daily devotional material. And through the HEAR journaling method, you'll learn how to Highlight, Explain, Apply, and Respond to passages, allowing for practical application.

The beginning

The book of Genesis describes what happened before anything but God existed, the world He created, and how man broke it.

But that's not the end of the story. In fact, it's just the beginning of many. This study will help you see how the threads of Genesis are woven through the entire Bible, including His plan to redeem this broken world.

This six-session Bible study is designed to help you:

- Lean how sin has broken the world

- See the God who loves and covenants with us

- Find hope in God's future plans